WILLIAM PERKINS

WILLIAM PERKINS

BY

JOEL R. BEEKE

AND

J. STEPHEN YUILLE

EP BOOKS

1st Floor Venture House, 6 Silver Court, Watchmead,
Welwyn Garden City, UK, AL7 1TS

www.epbooks.org
sales@epbooks.org

EP BOOKS are distributed in the USA by:
JPL Fulfillment
3741 Linden Avenue Southeast,
Grand Rapids, MI 49548.

E-mail: sales@jplfulfillment.com
Tel: 877.683.6935

First published 2015

ISBN: 978–1–78397–111–4

British Library Cataloguing in Publication Data available

CONTENTS

TIMELINE

1558	Mary dies; Elizabeth is crowned; Perkins is born
1559	*Act of Supremacy*; *Act of Uniformity*
1563	Foxe's *Book of Martyrs* is published
1570	Pope Pius V excommunicates Elizabeth; second edition of Foxe's *Book of Martyrs*
1571	The *39 Articles* are authorized by Parliament
1572	St. Bartholomew's Day massacre in France
1577	Perkins begins studies at Cambridge
1581	Perkins receives Bachelor's degree
1583	John Whitgift becomes Archbishop of Canterbury; his *Six Articles* insist on the 39 Articles, Book of Common Prayer, and royal supremacy
1584	Perkins receives Master's degree, is ordained to the ministry and appointed Fellow of Christ's College, Cambridge
1585	Perkins is appointed lecturer at Great St. Andrew's Church
1587	Mary Queen of Scots is executed
1588	Spanish Armada
1590	Perkins publishes *The Foundation of Christian Religion* and *A Golden Chain*
1590–91	Perkins serves as Dean of Christ's College, Cambridge

1595	Perkins marries Timothye Cradock
1597	Perkins publishes *A Reformed Catholic*
1598	Perkins publishes *A Treatise of Predestination*
1602	Perkins dies
1603	Elizabeth dies
1608–09	Perkins' *Works* are published in 3 volumes
1618–19	Synod of Dort

INTRODUCTION

Elizabeth I was one of England's most famous monarchs. She was born in 1533, as the fruit of that fateful union between Henry VIII and Anne Boleyn. In 1558, after the death of her Protestant half-brother, Edward, and the death of her Roman Catholic half-sister, Mary, she ascended the throne. She was immediately besieged from all sides. Domestically, she struggled with the religious establishment, and pursued a middle road between the various factions. Internationally, she had to contend with numerous enemies, culminating in the Spanish Armada's thwarted invasion in 1588. But Elizabeth withstood it all and turned England into the foremost Protestant power by the time of her death in 1603.

Elizabeth's forty-five year reign set the stage for the eventual formation of the British Empire, founded upon the sea. In the 1560s, Sir John Hawkins made three voyages down the African coastline, across the Atlantic to the Spanish colonies in the Americas, and eventually back to England. In the next decade, Sir Francis Drake also made three voyages to the West Indies. A few years later, the first English colony in America began at Roanoke (in modern-day North Carolina). During this period, spices arrived in England from India, silks from Turkey, and steel from Russia. More importantly, gold and silver from the New World began to line English coffers. Great commercial companies expanded their influence from Asia to America. London overtook Antwerp as the European capital of trade and finance.

Domestically, forges and furnaces appeared throughout the land. Glass and window industries boomed. Coal and copper production increased. The textile industry also flourished. The wealthy began to furnish their homes with curtains, tapestries, cushions, and cabinets. It was also a time of great educational opportunity. The number of grammar schools increased, while new colleges appeared and old colleges enlarged their enrollments. Closely related to this, interest in prose and poetry blossomed.

The life of William Perkins, one of England's most influential theologians, coincided with the years of Elizabeth's illustrious reign. Scholars have described him as "the principal architect of Elizabethan Puritanism," "the Puritan theologian of Tudor times," "the most important Puritan writer," "the prince of Puritan theologians," "the most famous of all Puritan divines," "the Puritan apostle," and "the father of Puritanism." Some have gone so far as to include him—along with John Calvin and Theodore Beza—in "the trinity of the orthodox." By the end of the sixteenth century, his writings had displaced in popularity those of the magisterial reformers.

Given Perkins's widespread popularity in his day and the subsequent century, it is strange that today relatively few people have heard of him. Why was he passed over when so many of the Puritan writers were reprinted in the nineteenth century? Why is he passed over in the majority of books and courses on church history? Why is this towering theologian one of England's least known? We do not pretend to have an answer. Perkins's relative obscurity remains one of the great puzzles of church history.

He was born to Thomas and Hannah Perkins in the village of Marston Jabbet (near Coventry) in Bulkington Parish of Warwickshire—the same county in which William Shakespeare was born six years later in 1564. Since no parish registers exist, it is impossible to trace Perkins's family ancestry. Was he part of a small or large family? What was his family's socio-economic status? Were they weavers, farmers, or perhaps merchants? What public and private events shaped his family's identity? Unfortunately, any details that might supply some insight into Perkins's formative years are lost to us.

We do know that he suffered from a deformity in his right hand. This must have presented a significant challenge for a young boy living in the world of plow and harness. Did his physical limitations leave him no alternative but to sharpen his cognitive capabilities? Or did he possess a natural aptitude and affinity for learning? Whatever the case might be, he demonstrated sufficient promise as a student that his family enrolled him in Christ's College, Cambridge, when he was nineteen years of age.

As Perkins strolled down Bridge Street over the River Cam to Christ's College, he immediately entered a world of fervor and ferment. The university had been a major player in the English Reformation. From 1511 to 1514, Desiderius Erasmus lectured in Greek while preparing his translation of the New Testament. Within ten years, William Tyndale prepared his English translation from Erasmus's text. By the 1520s, Martin Luther's works were circulating among scholars. In 1534, Cambridge accepted Parliament's Act of Supremacy, thus recognizing the king as the head of the Church of England. And, in 1549, the divinity chair was offered to Martin Bucer, thereby demonstrating the success of the Cambridge reformers. It was at this decidedly *Protestant* institution that Perkins began his life-long studies in June 1577 as a pensioner. A *pensioner* paid the commons—that is, the common expenses of the college. This fact suggests that socially his family stood on the borderline of the gentry.

Perkins quickly made a name for himself, but not for the reasons we might expect. Upon his arrival at Cambridge, "the wild fire of his youth began to break out," notes one biographer. He was entirely void of any interest in spiritual matters, and seemed wholly given to drunkenness and other vices. But, mercifully, God began to work in Perkins's heart, producing deep conviction for sin. Burdened by the weight of his sin, he turned to Christ, the Savior of sinners.

After receiving his master's degree in 1584, Perkins was ordained to the ministry. He immediately began preaching to the prisoners at Cambridge Castle. Perhaps he empathized with them, given his own experience of the gospel whereby God had liberated him from the prison cell of sin. Each Sunday, chained prisoners gathered in the nearby shire house to listen to Perkins as he proclaimed "deliverance to the captives." This ministry soon earned him the nick-name "the gaol birds' chaplain," but it did not last very long. Because of his growing popularity as a preacher, Perkins was appointed as lecturer at Great St.

Andrew's Church, located across from Christ's College. In his day, there was a great demand for educated men to serve as expositors of Scripture. The regular pastor assumed all other church responsibilities, thereby freeing the lecturer to focus exclusively on expounding God's Word. And so, for close to twenty years, Perkins preached from this pulpit to people from the town and university. In the words of one auditor, he was always "systematic, scholarly, solid, and simple" in his preaching.

Around the time of his appointment to Great St. Andrew's, Perkins was also elected to a fellowship at Christ's College. He held this position from 1584 to 1595, serving as Dean from 1590 to 1591. He chose to resign his place at Christ's College in 1595, in order to marry a young widow, Timothye Cradock. At the time, marriage and a university fellowship were deemed incompatible. During their seven years of marriage, they conceived seven children—three of whom died in infancy. What was Perkins's marriage like? What was he like as a husband and father? How did he and his wife cope with the death of three children? Regrettably, there is no diary or store of private letters to shed any light on these or any other personal matters.

Perkins struggled with kidney stones for many years. He finally succumbed to complications arising from this ailment in 1602 at age forty-four. Samuel Ward, one of Perkins's former students, penned in his diary:

> Consider the great blow given to the gospel of Christ by the death of Mr. Perkins. His life and doctrine did much good to the youth of the university, who held him in great esteem. He also did much good to many ministers in the country

through his advice and counsel. His life was upright and beyond reproach. He was very sparing in censuring others, very wise and discreet in his behavior, very humble and meek. During his final sickness, he was in great extremity by reason of the stone, yet he remained quiet and patient. When asked what he wanted, he answered, "Nothing but mercy." On Wednesday, October 2, when I was with him, he asked me to pray for him. God knows his death will be an irrecoverable loss and great judgment to the university, seeing as there is no-one to take his place.

Perkins's possessions were left to his wife, and a small amount was set aside for the poor. His body was buried at Great St. Andrew's Church at the expense of the university. Expressing the sentiment of many admirers throughout England, Perkins's closest friend, James Montagu, later Bishop of Winchester, preached the funeral sermon from Joshua 1:2, "Moses my servant is dead."

Admittedly, this brief introduction to the life of William Perkins leaves many questions unanswered. What was he like? What motivated him? What occupied his time and attention? What were his theological convictions? What contribution did he make to the advancement of the gospel in his day? What is his legacy? Our purpose in this book is to provide answers to these and other questions. We are not going to do so in typical fashion, that is, by providing a chronological overview of his life. Rather, we are going to approach our subject thematically. Drawing from his copious works and whatever fragmentary biographical details remain, we draw ten sketches of Perkins. Our prayer is that these will provide a faithful rendering of a man whose greatest desire was to "preach one Christ by Christ to the praise of Christ."

1

THE CONVERT

When Perkins enrolled at Christ's College, he was nineteen years old—slightly above the average age for a first year student. His family chose Laurence Chaderton (a reader in logic, and a well-known figure in the Puritan movement) as his personal tutor. Their choice of college and tutor points to their Puritan sympathies and, therefore, says something about Perkins's religious upbringing. Evidently, however, he had not personalized his family's faith by the time he attended his first lecture. His knowledge of God's truth was intellectual and theoretical at best, and fell well short of affecting his heart.

Perkins's indifference to the faith was clearly evident upon his arrival at the university. One biographer declares that Perkins "was profane and prodigal, and addicted to drunkenness." It is difficult to ascertain the full extent of his waywardness. Were these the sporadic indiscretions of a young man recently released from parental oversight, or the habitual indulgences of a young man wholly given to recklessness? Perkins's "profane and prodigal" life was further compounded by his interest in witchcraft. The exact nature of this dabbling is difficult to piece together. Was this open occultism or mere astrological speculation? In the words of one biographer, Perkins was addicted to the study of "natural magic, digging so deep in nature's mine to know the hidden causes and sacred qualities of things that some conceive that he bordered on hell itself in his curiosity. Beginning to be a practitioner in that black art, the blackness did not frighten him but the name of 'art' lured him to make himself its student." Reflecting on this predilection years later, Perkins wrote, "I long studied this art, and I was not quiet until I had seen all its secrets."

At some point during these early years at Cambridge, God began to work on Perkins's conscience. There is a particularly noteworthy incident in which he came face-to-face with his wretchedness: "As he was walking in the skirts of the town, he heard a woman say to a child that was forward and peevish, 'Hold your tongue, or I will give you to drunken Perkins yonder.'" Apparently, the words "drunken Perkins" so wounded him that he turned to the gospel for spiritual healing. The exact details of the story might very well be apocryphal, but Perkins's personal transformation was certainly real. Burdened with the weight of his sin, he turned to the Savior of sinners. As one historian observes:

> The happy hour arrived when the wandering sheep was brought home to the fold, and his vanity and wildness were turned into gravity and temperance ... When the roving parts and unstable conceits of this young scholar began to settle, and his studies were confined to and centered on divinity, he made incredible improvement in a very short time.

Perkins never shared any of the details of his conversion, but it seems safe to assume that his explanation of conversion as found in his writings reflects something of his understanding of what had happened to him personally. A case in point is his handling of Luke 6:47–48, where Christ proclaims, "Whosoever cometh to me, and heareth my sayings, and doeth them, I will shew you to whom he is like: he is like a man which built an house, and digged deep, and laid the foundation on a rock: and when the flood arose, the stream beat vehemently upon that house, and could not shake it: for it was founded upon a rock." According to Perkins, Christ here expounds the nature of true wisdom.

It consists, firstly, of *digging deep*. We dig deep, explains Perkins, when we "search and examine" our hearts, so that we discover the depth of our "iniquity." This is a necessary first step in conversion because we never trust in Christ alone for salvation until we are convinced of our need for Christ alone. In the building of this house, therefore, a "ransacking of the heart" must occur before the foundation is set. Surely, Perkins knew this from experience. Whether it was the warning of a frustrated mother to her misbehaving child or some other means, God had brought him face-to-face with his sin—not merely his drunkenness, but his all-pervading love of self. It horrified him. Yet it was the beginning of true wisdom, as it convinced him of his need for a Savior.

Secondly, true wisdom consists of *choosing a rock*. Perkins was adamant that our natural tendency is to look to ourselves for the grounds of salvation when, in reality, we must look away from ourselves. He firmly grasped the full import of Paul's declaration: "They are all under sin" (Romans 3:9). Once he began to dig deep, he realized that he was unable to heal himself. He saw that his sin touched his every thought, shaped his every desire, corrupted his every word, and tainted his every deed. In short, he recognized that he could contribute nothing to his salvation. Therefore, he chose the only rock that could provide protection against God's judgment: Jesus Christ.

Thirdly, true wisdom consists of *laying a foundation*. "Our salvation must be built on Christ," writes Perkins. "This is done by our faith in Christ, for as mutual love joins one man to another, so true faith makes us one with Christ." This union occurs when Christ takes hold of us by His Spirit, and we take hold of Christ by our faith. For Perkins, these are the bonds that knit us together with Christ in a union that links redemption accomplished and redemption applied. That is to say, all the blessings of salvation (all that Christ purchased for His people by His life and death) flow to us through our union with Him. Perkins understood that God justified him and sanctified him in Christ. He understood that he lived upon Christ's merit, communing with Him in His death, burial, and resurrection. For Perkins, this was the difference between feast and famine; fullness and emptiness; heaven and hell.

Christ makes it clear that, in sharp contrast to the wise man, the foolish man builds his house upon the sand: "But he that heareth, and doeth not, is like a man that without a foundation built an house upon the earth; against which the stream did beat vehemently, and immediately it fell; and the ruin of that house was great" (Luke 6:49). In Perkins's handling of this verse, he affirmed that both the wise man and the foolish man profess to know Christ. This is evident from the fact that their buildings are identical. What distinguishes the two men is not the house they build, but the foundation upon which they build: the foolish man chooses the sand, whereas the wise man chooses the rock. For Perkins, these two foundations represent the difference between head (speculative or notional) knowledge and heart (sensible and inclinational) knowledge. With this distinction in view, he declares, "Knowledge in the brain will not save the soul. Saving knowledge in religion is experimental. Whoever is truly founded upon Christ feels the power and efficacy of His death and resurrection, effectually causing the death of sin and the life of grace, which both appear in new obedience."

Prior to his conversion as a student at Christ's College, Perkins was the foolish man. It is highly likely that he was raised in a Christian home. Without question, he was catechized in his parish church on Sunday afternoons and, therefore, familiar with the church's doctrine and tradition. But his knowledge of divine truth was merely notional. It never touched his heart. But the moment arrived when God began to work upon Perkins. As a result, he saw his sin as he had never seen it before. He became convinced of his inability to please God, and this caused him to look for a Savior. In a word, Christ took hold of Perkins by His Spirit, and Perkins took hold of Christ by his faith. By virtue of this union, he understood himself to stand accepted by God in Christ—a solid foundation indeed.

2

THE THEOLOGIAN

From the day of his conversion to the day of his death (a little over twenty years), Perkins devoted himself to the study of Scripture. He produced close to fifty books—either published by him or compiled and published by his friends after his death. These included expositions of Galatians 1–5, Matthew 5–7, Hebrews 11, Jude, and Revelation 1–3; discourses on various cases of conscience; and treatises on worship, preaching, assurance, predestination, the Apostles' Creed, the Lord's Prayer, and the errors of the Roman Catholic Church.

These writings demonstrate the depth of Perkins's learning and the breadth of his reading. According to one account, he "perused books so speedily that one would think he read nothing, yet so accurately that one would think he read everything." This is a rare gift indeed—the ability to digest books quickly while providing an exact account of their content. But what made up Perkins's staple diet?

At Cambridge, the regular arts course consisted of the *trivium* (grammar, rhetoric, logic), the *quadrivium* (music, arithmetic, geometry, astronomy), and the philosophies (natural, moral, metaphysical). Once students completed the bachelor's and master's degrees, they proceeded to the higher faculties such as law, theology, and medicine. Since the time of Augustine, it was believed that these arts and philosophies provided the necessary foundation for theological study. Perkins's familiarity with the works of the moralists, historians, and philosophers is prevalent throughout his writings.

Of particular note is Perkins's predilection for Peter Ramus's *Ars Logica*. Laurence Chaderton first introduced Ramus to Cambridge students in the 1560s. Ramus (1515– 1572), a convert from Roman Catholicism, proposed a single logic to simplify all academic subjects. The task of the logician was to classify concepts in order to make them understandable and memorable. For Ramus, this was accomplished through method—the orderly presentation of a subject according to parts and divisions. His method quickly won the support of many scholars, including Gabriel Harvey—a lecturer who used it to reform the arts curriculum. Harvey's presentation deeply impressed Perkins, whose works clearly demonstrate his predilection for division and classification.

Perkins's writings reveal not only his proficiency in the arts and philosophies, but the depth of his reading within a wide theological spectrum. Unsurprisingly, Augustine stands out from among the Patristics. Perkins also referred frequently to Jerome, Polycarp, and Cyprian. Many of the Scholastics and Romanists figure prominently, especially in his polemical works. Most noteworthy, however, is

Perkins's familiarity with the Reformers. He referred to John Calvin as "that worthy instrument of the gospel," and cited his *Institutes* and *Commentaries*. However, Calvin was not the only stream from which Perkins drank. From among Reformed scholars, he also quoted Theodore Beza, Jerome Zanchius, Zacharias Ursinus, Caspar Olevianus, Franciscus Junius, and Augustinus Marloratus. And, from among Lutheran scholars, he made reference to Martin Luther, Philipp Melanchthon, Victorinus Strigel, Martinus Chemnitius, Niels Hemingsen, Matthias Illyricus, and Andreas Hyperius. Additionally, Perkins appealed to the writings of English Reformers such as William Tyndale, John Bradford, and Hugh Latimer.

Perkins was not a slavish disciple of any of these authors. He rejected any appeal to Patristics, Scholastics, or Reformers as authoritative, insisting that we should closely examine "the ancient writers" and accept them as long as they agree with "the writings of the prophets and apostles." Perkins was prepared to draw from any author who could help him expound Scripture. "Although the best men's works," says he, "are but base stuff in comparison to the pure Word of God, yet we must not condemn the writings of holy men, but read them in their place to furnish and enable us in the study of Scripture. Whoever holds or practices the contrary knows not what light these holy men might yield upon many dark places of Scripture."

While Perkins was a student at Christ's College, Chaderton had instituted a program of studies that emphasized the study of Scripture, including mastery of Hebrew and Greek. Perkins participated in this Bible-centered course of study, which consisted of comparing Scripture with Scripture, then Scripture with "the ancient writers." This approach remained with him throughout his life. At every turn, he championed what he called Scripture's "infallible certainty," meaning "the testimony of Scripture is the testimony of God Himself." Because Scripture is the very Word of God, Perkins viewed it as the means by which God reveals Himself and imparts grace to His people. This necessarily implied that Scripture must stand alone at the center of the life of the Christian and the church. Owing to this, he adopted Scripture as the axiom of all his thinking and the focus of all his teaching. Unsurprisingly, his adherence to the absolute authority of Scripture shaped his theology.

When delving into the specifics of Perkins's theology, we must maintain sight of his fundamental perspectives concerning the authority of Scripture, the majesty of God, the centrality of Christ, the beauty of grace, the reality of eternity, the unity of life, and the efficacy of the gospel. We must also remain sensitive to his conviction that "theology is the science of living blessedly forever." This conviction runs like an undercurrent beneath all his writings. According to Perkins, the mind is the supreme faculty of the soul. In making this assertion, he was not suggesting that the will necessarily follows the dictates of the mind. Rather, in referring to the mind as the supreme faculty of the soul, he intended to convey the reality that the knowledge of God always begins in the mind because the will cannot choose what the mind does not know. He remarks, "The mind must approve and give assent before the will can choose or will; and when the mind has no power to conceive or give assent, then the will has no power to will." That being the case, the goal of all theology is to engage the mind with the ultimate purpose of embracing the heart's innermost affections. For Perkins, theology was neither a mere intellectual exercise nor a mere academic pursuit, but the means by which we grow in acquaintance with God and consequently in godliness, thereby making it "the science of living blessedly forever."

Perkins viewed the pursuit of blessedness as fundamental to man's existence. The ancient Stoics maintained that blessedness was found in indifference—the impassionate acceptance of circumstances. We must learn to desire *what is*. When we do, we rise above the perturbations of life to experience blessedness. The ancient Epicureans, on the other hand, affirmed that blessedness is found in indulgence—the gratification of desires. For Epicurus, there were two kinds of pleasure, stemming from two kinds of desire: natural and vain. In short, we must learn to satisfy our natural desires while denying our vain desires. When we do, we experience true peace of mind. These two, Stoicism and Epicureanism, have epitomized man's pursuit of blessedness throughout history. But they merely serve to reveal the futility of man's pursuit, in that they show that man always proceeds on a faulty premise: the notion that blessedness lies in externals.

For his part, Perkins was adamant that blessedness is not a carnal joy arising from our circumstances, but a spiritual joy arising from our relationship with God. In other words, blessedness is rooted in an unchanging God, not changing circumstances. Perkins affirmed that God is most perfect—one simple, indivisible essence. This makes Him very different from us. We are not simple beings, but consist of parts: body and soul. In turn, our body consists of parts: skin, blood, arms, legs, bones, ligaments, tendons, organs, etc. Our soul also consists of parts: understanding, will, memory, and conscience. These, in turn, bear qualities such as intelligence, wisdom, and emotions.

But God is a simple being, incapable of the least division. That means it is impossible to distinguish anything within God's essence. His attributes, therefore, are not parts of His essence, but are essential properties of His total and complete essence. His attributes can no more be separated from Him than He can be separated from Himself. Therefore, God is not merely wise; He is wisdom. He is not merely powerful; He is power. He is not merely good; He is goodness. He is not merely holy; He is holiness. He is not merely just; He is justice. While they are distinguished in their objects and effects, God's attributes are all one in Him.

Since God is a perfect being, He is necessarily sufficient and satisfied in Himself. That being the case, He is the source of all good. If He is the source of all good, then He is the only source of our blessedness; that is to say, we find our greatest good in communion with Him. For Perkins, therefore, blessedness is simply a "condition" whereby we enjoy "fellowship with God."

But how do we enter this "condition"? Perkins believed the answer was found in the Beatitudes (Matthew 5:3–10), which he expounded as eight "rules" of blessedness. The first "rule" is poverty of spirit: "Blessed are the poor in spirit: for theirs is the kingdom of heaven." According to Perkins, Christ is here describing an attitude of heart that arises from a proper self-perception before God. We perceive our sin and, as a result, recognize that we are without moral virtues adequate to commend ourselves to God. Consequently, we are aware of our utter dependence upon God's grace. Perkins described this attitude of heart as follows: "Finding no goodness in their hearts, they despair in themselves, and flee wholly to the mercy of God in Christ for grace and comfort."

The second "rule" of blessedness is sorrow: "Blessed are they that mourn: for they shall be comforted." This sorrow is "grievous distress" accompanied by "an inward feeling" of spiritual want. At this point, Perkins was careful to distinguish between two kinds of sorrow: carnal and spiritual. The first is *ungodly* sorrow, which arises from the negative consequences associated with sin. We see it in the likes of Esau, Saul, and Judas. The second is *godly* sorrow, which arises from a sight of our sin as committed against a glorious God. Another word for this is repentance.

The third "rule" of blessedness is meekness: "Blessed are the meek: for they shall inherit the earth." Perkins defines meekness as "a gift of God's Spirit whereby a man moderates his affection for anger, and bridles his impatience, hatred, and desire for revenge." It arises out of the first two Beatitudes. The poor in spirit know they are sinful. This sight of sin leads to sorrow which, in turn, leads to meekness. We realize that God has the right to do with us as He pleases. To put it another way, we recognize that our worst circumstance is better than what we deserve.

The fourth "rule" of blessedness is longing for righteousness: "Blessed are they which do hunger and thirst after righteousness: for they shall be filled." This righteousness is twofold: outward "whereby a sinner is justified through grace in Christ, and so stands righteous before God"; and inward "whereby a man is sanctified and made holy, having God's image renewed in him by the

Spirit of grace." To hunger and thirst after righteousness, therefore, is to desire both justification (righteousness imputed) and sanctification (righteousness imparted). As for the actual act of "hungering and thirsting," Perkins believed Christ was speaking of a condition resulting from "grief of heart" over our unrighteousness. When we perceive the seriousness of our sin, we become poor in spirit. The result is sorrow and meekness, which lead to "an earnest and constant desire for the righteousness of God."

The fifth "rule" of blessedness is mercy: "Blessed are the merciful: for they shall obtain mercy." Perkins defines mercy as "a holy compassion of heart, whereby a man is moved to help another in his misery." Mindful of the body, we seek to alleviate people's physical suffering. We meet their "outward necessity for food, raiment, etc." Mindful of the soul, we seek to alleviate people's spiritual suffering. We are "careful for the salvation of others, using means to bring people from spiritual darkness to light, from the power of Satan to God, from the state of sin and danger of hell to the state of grace in true faith and repentance, and so life eternal."

The sixth "rule" of blessedness is purity in heart: "Blessed are the pure in heart: for they shall see God." For Perkins, the pure in heart are "purged from the defilement of their sins, and are in part renewed and sanctified by the Holy

Spirit." The Holy Spirit effects this renewal by "creating in the mind a saving faith, which unites a man unto Christ," by "mortifying all the corruptions in the mind, will, and affections," and by "putting into it inward holiness whereby the image of Christ is renewed." Perkins was careful to stress that the "measure" of this renewal is only "in part" in this life, for sanctification is not completed until death. Those, however, in whom the renewal has begun are already reckoned "pure in heart" in God's sight.

The seventh "rule" of blessedness is peacemaking: "Blessed are the peacemakers: for they shall be called the children of God." "By peace," writes Perkins, "we must understand concord and agreement between man and man." As peacemakers, we attempt to "make peace between God and man" through the gospel, for Christ has given us "the ministry of reconciliation." We also seek to keep the peace among others. "When God's Spirit works in us peace of conscience towards God in Christ," says Perkins, "He also moves us to seek peace with all men, and to make peace between those who are at variance." Those who are proud, discontent, and resentful, cause discord wherever they go. However, those who are at peace with God keep the peace, seeking to extinguish anger, strife, and division.

The eighth "rule" of blessedness is persecution: "Blessed are they which are persecuted for righteousness' sake: for theirs is the kingdom of heaven." According to Perkins, we suffer persecution "for the sake of righteousness" when we suffer "for professing, believing, and maintaining the doctrine of the gospel taught by Christ touching remission of sins and life everlasting." The world admires the self-confident, not the poor in spirit; it admires the lighthearted, not the sorrowful; it admires the proud, not the meek; it admires the shameless, not the righteous; it admires the avenger, not the merciful; it admires the self-indulgent, not the pure in heart; and it admires the aggressor, not the peacemaker. In short, the world despises Christ and, therefore, it persecutes all who are like Him.

Significant in Perkins's eyes is the fact that Christ begins and concludes these eight "rules" of blessedness with the phrase "kingdom of heaven" (Matthew 5:3, 10). This necessarily implies that the promises found in the Beatitudes belong to all those who are part of God's kingdom. When speaking of this kingdom, Perkins differentiated between the present kingdom of grace and the future kingdom of glory. These two aspects of the kingdom do not differ in "substance," but in "degree," in that the kingdom of grace is the beginning of the kingdom of glory. We are blessed, therefore, because we possess the present kingdom of grace and one day we will enjoy the future kingdom of glory.

Focusing on the "blessedness" of the present kingdom of grace, Perkins appeals to Romans 14:17, where Paul declares, "For the kingdom of God is not meat and drink; but righteousness, and peace, and joy in the Holy Ghost." Here, Paul mentions three components of the kingdom: "righteousness," "peace," and "joy." Regarding this, Perkins remarks, "When God's Spirit rules in a man's heart, then first he is justified; secondly, he has peace with God; and, thirdly, he has the joy of the Holy Spirit, who is an unspeakable comfort, far surpassing all earthly joy." And "these three," according to Perkins, "notably set out the state of a happy man."

Turning his attention to the "blessedness" of the future kingdom of glory, Perkins focuses on the beatific vision: "Blessed are the pure in heart: for they shall see God." For Perkins, this "vision" is not a sight of God's essence. We cannot see God because there is no "proportion" between a human eye and that which is infinite and invisible (1 Timothy 6:16). The promise must, therefore, refer to a "sight of the mind"—when we see God so far forth as our mind is capable. In one sense, we see God right now through the eyes of faith, but Perkins affirmed that this sight is nothing in comparison to what is coming. At present, we see God "by His effects," namely, His works of creation, providence, and redemption; but in the future we will see Him "perfectly." At glorification, we will be like Christ and therefore able to commune with God to the fullest capacities of our souls. There will be nothing to hinder our enjoyment of Him. This will result in hitherto unknown delight as we rest fully and finally in Him. For Perkins, "this seeing of God" will be "true happiness."

In many respects, this blessedness is the *sine qua non* of Perkins's theology. Blessedness is every man's longing. The problem is that most people do not know where it is found, nor do they understand the way to attain it. Perkins was convinced that being spiritual we can only be satisfied by a spiritual good, and being eternal we can only be satisfied by an eternal good. We are only blessed, therefore, when we take God as our chief good, for He alone is originally, supremely, infinitely, and eternally good. "Happy is that people, whose God is the LORD" (Psalm 144:15).

3

THE REFORMER

The Reformation in England was a long and drawn out process, encompassing much of the sixteenth and seventeenth centuries. It began with Henry VIII, who initiated a power struggle with Rome, which came to a head when Parliament passed the Supremacy Act by which Henry was declared "the only supreme head in earth of the Church of England." This Act focused on the authority of the pope, not the doctrines of the Roman Catholic Church. At heart, Henry still accepted many of Catholicism's practices, as is evident in the Six Articles passed by Parliament in 1539. They condemned all who opposed transubstantiation, vows of chastity, private masses, and auricular confession, and all who supported the giving of the cup to the laity and the marriage of the clergy. There were those, however, who disagreed with these Six Articles, viewing the Reformation as much more than freedom from papal intrusion into domestic affairs. Therefore, from the outset, the English Reformation actually embraced two distinct tendencies. The first was semi-Roman while the other was anti-Roman. This division was clearly apparent during the reigns of Edward and Mary, as England wavered between Catholicism and Protestantism, and it continued well into the reign of Elizabeth.

When Elizabeth ascended the throne, the majority of England's population was still inclined to Catholicism. This was evident in the revolt of the northern earls in the early years of her reign. As for the Roman Catholic Church's official position regarding Elizabeth, it was uncompromising: she was illegitimate and thus unfit to rule. Her position was made even more precarious by the fact that her relative, Mary Stuart, queen of Scotland, had her eyes fixed on the English throne. As the great-grand-daughter of Henry VII, she had a legitimate claim. This was strengthened by her marriage to Henry Stuart, Lord Darnley, the grandson of Henry VIII's sister, Margaret. Both were committed Catholics. Therefore, they posed a legitimate threat to Elizabeth, as the Catholics of England considered them their proper monarchs. Mary engaged in ongoing plots to snatch the throne from Elizabeth until she finally met the executioner's axe in 1587.

This political intrigue was compounded by the pope's meddling in England's internal affairs. In 1570, Pius V issued a papal bull, excommunicating Elizabeth as a tyrant and heretic. It branded "the pretended queen of England" as "the servant of iniquity," and it made her a legitimate target for assassination. The pope guaranteed an immediate passage to heaven for whoever dared to carry out his design. Interestingly, this same year marked the release of the second edition of John Foxe's *Book of Martyrs*, originally published in 1563. It emerged but a few months after the papal bull. In the words of one cleric, it was a "work of great importance ... being very profitable in bringing Her Majesty's subjects to a good opinion, understanding, and liking of the present government." Foxe offered a vivid account of those who were martyred during the reign of Bloody Mary. In so doing, he portrayed the English Reformation during Elizabeth's reign as the restoration of Christ's church, which had been concealed for centuries under the dark cloak of Roman Catholicism. His book served to galvanize opposition to Rome. At this time, it became commonplace for English theologians to interpret their Reformation as an apocalyptic event heralding the fall of antichrist—the pope. Foxe's *Book of Martyrs* went through another three editions during Elizabeth's reign, and became the most popular book after the Bible.

The Roman Catholic threat was further heightened on St. Bartholomew's Day, August 24, 1572, when Parisian mobs murdered thousands of defenseless Huguenots. The bells rang in celebration in Rome, as Pope Gregory walked from shrine to shrine in grateful procession. The English viewed the gruesome massacre as a prelude to a coming assault. Two years later, the first Catholic priests trained at a seminary in the Spanish Netherlands arrived on England's shores. They were followed by six hundred more before the turn of the century. Their mission was to minister to the faithful while opposing the claims of an excommunicated monarch. Within a few years of the arrival of the first priests, Jesuits also made their way to England. The pope had established the Jesuit order for one simple reason—to combat the Reformation. These "black horsemen of the pope" infiltrated English society for the expressed purpose of restoring the old religion.

Perkins would have been well aware of these political and religious machinations—each popish plot was the topic of anxious conversation. Realizing that the English Reformation was far from secure, he was determined to defend the church in its ongoing conflict with Rome. He was convinced that Roman Catholicism had wandered so far from the teaching of Scripture that it had lost the true knowledge of Christ. Simply put, it had become so synergistic in its understanding of the gospel that it obscured the full extent of man's sin and God's grace. Consequently, it was not merely one of several acceptable Christian traditions; on the contrary, it was the "great whore" of Revelation 17.

Unsurprisingly, many of Perkins's writings reflect this conflict. In one of his most well-known, *A Reformed Catholic*, he makes it clear that "union of the two religions can never be made, any more than the union of light and darkness." By way of explanation, he adds, "Although the Catholics honor Christ in their words, they turn Him into a pseudo-Christ and an idol of their own brains." In this treatise, Perkins addressed twenty-two issues dividing Protestants and Catholics. Interestingly, the first six were related directly to the doctrines of grace: free will, original sin, assurance, justification, merit, and satisfaction.

The most important of these was the meaning of free will. Like Martin Luther and John Calvin before him, Perkins understood the struggle with Roman Catholicism as hinging upon a biblical understanding of free will. The Roman Catholics contended, according to Perkins, that "a man's will works by itself and by its own natural power along with God's grace in the first conversion of a sinner." Perkins countered that, when it comes to conversion, a man's will does not work by itself but by God's grace alone.

Undoubtedly, his conviction regarding the role of man's will in conversion reflected his own perceived experience. As he recalled his early years at Christ's College, he saw a young man with absolutely no interest in spiritual matters. Suddenly, his inclination was turned heavenward. Perkins could not account for this radical transformation apart from God's sovereign grace. His will had not acted by "its own natural power," but solely by God's grace.

Perkins's position was rooted in his understanding of the image of God in man. He maintained that this image originally consisted of natural gifts (mind, affections, and will) and supernatural gifts (knowledge, righteousness, and holiness). When Adam sinned in the Garden of Eden, what happened? His natural gifts were corrupted, and his supernatural gifts were removed. This has been man's condition ever since.

In his "created" state, man's will possessed "liberty of nature, in which he could will either good or evil." In his "corrupted" state, this "liberty of nature" remains; however, it is now "joined with a necessity of sinning because it stands in bondage under sin." "In this respect," adds Perkins, "it is fitly termed by Augustine: 'the bound will.'" In his "created" state, therefore, man possessed free will: the freedom to choose what he wanted. In his "corrupted" state, man still possesses this freedom. The problem, however, is that his mind is darkened and his affections are hardened, because he is excluded from the life of God

(Ephesians 4:17–18). Consequently, his will is controlled by a mind that prefers darkness to light and by affections that prefer evil to good. As a result, his free will itself is now a "bound will." All that to say, we are free to will; however, we do so with a will enslaved to sin.

This means that even when we exercise our natural gifts (mind, affections, and will) in choosing what is good, we fail to do so from a right principle. The supernatural gifts (knowledge, righteousness, and holiness) are gone and, therefore, we are unable to choose what is good for the only motive that is acceptable to God, namely, His glory. Perkins states, "A man without supernatural grace might contribute alms, execute justice, speak truth, etc., which are good things considered in themselves since God has commanded them. But he cannot do them well. The good thing done by a natural man is sin in respect of the doer, because it fails both for its right beginning (faith unfeigned) and for its right end (the glory of God)."

Perkins's position on free will was not new to the English church, but reflected the Thirty-Nine Articles of Religion:

> The condition of man after the fall of Adam is such, that he cannot turn and prepare himself, by his own natural strength and good works, to faith and calling upon God: Wherefore we have no power to do good works pleasant and acceptable to God, without the grace of God by Christ preventing us, that we may have a good will, and working with us, when we have that good will (Article 10).

This was a key issue during the Reformation. As a matter of fact, some scholars believe it was the main issue. The Roman Catholic Church had developed an exaggerated concept of the role of man's will in salvation.

The Reformers, on the other hand, insisted that we are so captivated by sin that we have no power to escape from it. Because of original sin, the will (though free in the actions it performs) is captive in its way of performing them. This difference in perspective was fundamental. If, according to the Roman Catholic view, God's grace simply assists man's nature, then the church's primary concern is to challenge people to use their free will. If, on the other hand, man's nature is useless apart from God's grace, then the church's chief calling is to ensure that people understand their complete dependence upon God's grace for salvation.

This fundamental difference on the nature of free will directly impacted the debate surrounding the doctrine of justification. Perkins branded Roman Catholicism "an enemy of the grace of God because it exalts the liberty of man's will, and extenuates the grace of God, and joins the merit of works as a concurring cause with the grace of God in the procurement of eternal life." If our will works in conversion "by itself and by its own natural power along with God's grace," then the implication for the doctrine of justification is self-evident. For Roman Catholics, justification is preceded by a preparation "which is an action wrought partly by the Holy Spirit and partly by the power of natural free will whereby a man disposes himself to his own future justification." Justification itself has two parts. The first is God's act whereby He grants "the pardon of sin" and "the infusion of inward righteousness." The second is man's act whereby he does good works, thus becoming "more just and righteous."

Perkins's understanding of free will was incompatible with such a view of justification. Because the supernatural gifts (knowledge, righteousness, holiness) were lost at the fall, our will is in bondage to sin, and we are incapable of good works. Justification, therefore, cannot include our works of righteousness. We are completely dependent on a righteousness that is not our own. For Perkins, this is Christ's righteousness. He asserted that "the obedience of Christ is made the righteousness of every believer, not by infusion, but by imputation." In other words, God accepts Christ's merit as if it were our own.

Pivotal to Perkins's understanding of justification was his covenant theology. He taught that, in the Garden of Eden, God established the covenant of works with Adam and his posterity. That is to say, Adam stood in the place of his physical descendants, and God gave him a specific commandment. When Adam sinned, God counted his sin as his posterity's sin, his guilt as his posterity's guilt, and his punishment as his posterity's punishment. This gave rise to the need for another covenant—the covenant of grace. Adam has a counterpart—the last Adam (Christ). Just as Adam's "offence" resulted in death and condemnation for his posterity, so too Christ's "gift by grace" resulted in life and justification for his posterity (Romans 5:15–19). For Perkins, when we believe, we are no longer in Adam (under the covenant of works), because we have been united with Christ (under the covenant of grace), who has fulfilled the covenant of works on our behalf. This is the framework for Perkins's understanding of "mutual imputation"—Christ fulfills the covenant of works, meeting its requirement by His active obedience (life) and paying its penalty by His passive obedience (death).

According to Perkins, therefore, justification is the act of God "whereby such as believe are accounted just before God through the obedience of Christ." When God justifies us, He charges our sin to Christ, who died as our substitute, bearing the curse of the law on our behalf. Because our sin is charged to Christ, God forgives us our sin. And when God justifies us, He credits Christ's righteousness to us. Christ lived as our substitute, fulfilling the law on our behalf. On this basis, God declares us to be righteous. Again, Perkins's position was faithful to the Thirty-Nine Articles of Religion, which state: "We are accounted righteous before God, only for the merit of our Lord and Savior Jesus Christ, by faith, and not for our own works or deservings" (Article 11).

During the early years of Elizabeth's reign, many Roman Catholics left England. Among them were professors of divinity, and many university fellows. Once upon the Continent, they gathered themselves in English academic communities. Their stated goal was to support their fellow Catholics in England while seeking to win back the country for Rome. One of the most influential of these Elizabethan exiles was William Bishop. He was educated at Oxford, Rome, and Paris, and he was a member of the Catholic missions to England. He responded to Perkins's *Reformed Catholic*:

> I took it in hand to confute this book, not only because a friend of good intelligence requested me to do so, but because, having perused it, I found it more scholarly than what the Protestants usually produce. For starters, the points of controversy are set down distinctly and, for the most part, truly. Afterward, the chief arguments are produced from the Scriptures, fathers, and reason. Although he does not name them, his arguments are culled out of Luther, Calvin, Kemnitius, Peter Martyr, and such like. Lastly, he raises some objections made in favor of the Catholic doctrine,

and answers them as well as he can. I speak this to his commendation: I have not seen any book of like quantity published by a Protestant that contains more matter or employs a better method. Before the printing of my confutation was finished, I heard that Mr. Perkins was dead. I am sorry that this comes forth too late to do him any good. Yet, since his work lives to poison others, my confutation is never the less necessary to act as a preservative against it.

It is doubtful that Perkins's polemic against Rome influenced any of his most ardent opponents like Bishop. But that was never his principal aim. He was chiefly concerned about the condition of the English church, which was still struggling to rid itself of the remnants of the old religion. In this sense, he accomplished his desired goal. He succeeded in proving to his fellow countrymen that the Church of England had reformed medieval teaching in the light of Scripture. He also succeeded in demonstrating to them how their doctrine differed fundamentally from that of Roman Catholicism. Without a doubt, his engagement in the English Reformation went a long way to convince others "to ascribe all the good we have or can do wholly to the grace of God."

4

THE POLEMICIST

While struggling against the Roman Catholic Church, Perkins also engaged in several controversies related to the Church of England's own doctrine. These were connected to important questions regarding the nature of grace, especially as it relates to the doctrine of predestination. The Thirty-Nine Articles of Religion expressed the thinking of the key leaders within the Elizabethan church:

> Predestination to life is the everlasting purpose of God, whereby (before the foundations of the world were laid) He has constantly decreed by His counsel secret to us, to deliver from curse and damnation those whom He has chosen in Christ out of mankind, and to bring them by Christ to everlasting salvation, as vessels made to honor (Article 17).

Those who are chosen are subsequently called "according to God's purpose." This calling entails a series of steps:

> They through grace obey the calling: they be justified freely: they be made sons of God by adoption: they be made

like the image of His only-begotten Son Jesus Christ: they walk religiously in good works, and at length, by God's mercy, they attain to everlasting felicity (Article 17).

This was, therefore, the standard teaching on God's grace within the Church of England in Perkins's day. However, there were dissenting voices. Upon his arrival in England, Peter Baro, a French Huguenot and former student of John Calvin, was appointed the Lady Margaret's Professor of Divinity at Cambridge. In 1579, he began to question the prevailing theology of grace. He objected to the notion that "the eternal decree of God" concerning salvation "affects and accomplishes all things." He argued that God's work of predestination is based upon His foreknowledge of our faith and works. Unsurprisingly, Baro's position caused a stir among the likes of Laurence Chaderton (Master of Emmanuel College) and William Whitaker (Master of St. John's College). It also caught the attention of a second-year student, who was sure to have heard Baro's views expressed in lectures and sermons.

For Perkins, the idea that God's predestination is based upon His foreknowledge of our faith and works undermined the very nature of God's grace, and contradicted the church's official position on the subject. In 1590, he entered the debate with *A Golden Chain* (*Armilla Aurea*), in which he openly challenged Baro's position. His expressed desire was that his treatise would serve as a "mite" in the Church of England's "theological treasury."

In the preface, he identified four views on predestination. The first is Pelagianism, which "placed the cause of God's predestination in man." In other words, God chooses people on the basis of what He foresees in them. For

Perkins, Baro was nothing more than a new Pelagian. The second view is Lutheranism, which affirmed that God purposed "to choose some to salvation of His mere mercy, without any respect of their faith, or good works." He purposed to reject the rest, because they would "reject His grace offered them in the gospel." The third view is Semi-Pelagianism, which ascribed "God's predestination, partly to mercy, and partly to men's foreseen preparations and meritorious works." Perkins believed this was essentially the Roman Catholic position. The fourth view is the Reformed, according to which "the cause of the execution of God's predestination is His mercy in Christ in those who are saved; and the fall and corruption of man in those who perish."

Obviously, Perkins placed himself in the fourth camp, affirming that "God's decree in as much as it concerns man is called predestination, which is the decree of God by which He has ordained all men to a certain and everlasting estate, that is, either to salvation or condemnation, for His own glory." For Perkins, God executes His decree through four "degrees." The first is effectual calling whereby "a sinner, being severed from the world, is entertained into God's family." The second is justification whereby "such as believe are accounted just before God through the obedience of Christ Jesus." The third is sanctification whereby "such as believe, being delivered from the tyranny of sin, are little by little renewed in holiness and righteousness." The fourth is glorification whereby the saints are perfectly transformed "into the image of the Son of God." This "golden chain" constituted, for Perkins, the definitive statement on God's grace. In a word, our sin is so pervasive that nothing but God's sovereign grace can overcome it.

Perkins was well aware of the objections raised against the Reformed doctrine of predestination. The most troubling was the contention that it made God the author of sin. Perkins countered by affirming that God decrees everything that comes to pass; however, He is not the author of evil because He moves second causes to act freely in accordance with their desires. Another way of saying this is that God is the first cause (motion) and man is the second cause (motive) of all actions. In the production of every effect, therefore, there is an efficiency of two causes: first and second.

Further to this, Perkins believed "there are two branches" in the execution of God's decree; namely, "His operation, and His operative permission." By an act of His will, God decrees everything that comes to pass, but He does so in two ways. By a *positive* decree, He wills that which is good, and He effects the good that He decrees. By a *privative* decree, He wills that which is evil, and He willingly permits the evil He decrees. Perkins illustrated the difference between the two by appealing to Joseph. His brothers sold him into slavery in Egypt. Was this evil? Yes. But, in keeping with Scripture, Perkins affirmed that it was God who sent Joseph into Egypt (Genesis 45:8). That is to say, God decreed it. Does this make God the author of evil? For Perkins, the answer is *no*, because God decreed it by a privative decree. He executed His decree by "His operative permission."

Baro was unconvinced, and he openly attacked Perkins's position. He launched into a defense of "universal election," according to which election and reprobation are based entirely on God's foreknowledge of our future decisions about Christ. This time, Baro was forced out of Cambridge.

As a result of the controversy, William Whitaker submitted articles to the Archbishop of Canterbury, John Whitgift, designed to resolve the debate once for all. These became known as the Lambeth Articles. They emphasized a Reformed doctrine of predestination, asserting that the cause of predestination is "only the will of the good pleasure of God." Elizabeth, however, was uneasy with the articles because she believed they delved into matters "tender and dangerous to weak ignorant minds." For this reason, she exercised her royal supremacy by refusing to authorize them.

Perkins produced his own response in 1598 with *A Treatise of Predestination*. His chief concern was to defend the Reformed doctrine of predestination against its detractors by demonstrating the "consensus and concord" among past theologians. He also wanted to respond to the criticism that the Reformed view resulted in fatalistic determinism. Generally speaking, there are two main schools of thought on the nature of free will: *indeterminism* and *determinism*. The first maintains that our will is free from internal motives and desires; in other words, it is free from our mind's thoughts and our heart's affections. That means it possesses arbitrary power: we do not know why it chooses what it chooses. The second school of thought maintains that our will is not free from internal motives and desires; in other words, it is not free from our mind's thoughts and our heart's affections. That means it does not possess arbitrary power: we do know why it chooses what it chooses. As far as Perkins was concerned, our will is in bondage to our own corrupt faculties—a darkened mind and hardened heart (Ephesians 4:18). This means that our will does not possess arbitrary power; on the contrary, it follows the dictates of misplaced affections. But Perkins was careful to assert that this does not undermine self-determination because it maintains a difference between *constraining* and *non-constraining* causes. We are free because our choices are our own, but our choices are not free from our darkened mind and hardened heart. In a word, we possess a free will that is in bondage to sin.

It was to this specific work that Jacob Arminius replied in *An Examination of Perkins's Little Book on the Order and Mode of Predestination*, writing:

> When I observed that it bore your name, which was already well known to me by previously published works of high character, I thought that I must diligently read and consider it, and see whether you, who are devoted to the most accurate learning, could remove the difficulties which have long disquieted my mind. I, therefore, read it once and again with impartiality, as far as I could, and with candor, as you desire. But, in reading, I perceived that all my difficulties were not removed by your work.

Arminius labeled Perkins as one of those who did "not fear to add to the Scriptures whatever they think proper, and are accustomed to attribute as much as possible to their own conceptions which they style natural ideas." In other words, he contended that Perkins had moved beyond Scripture into the realm of philosophical speculation. Arminius's reply was not published until 1612, by which time both he and Perkins were buried. But some of his followers produced the *Remonstrance*, in which they defended Arminius's position. The Dutch Calvinists regarded these ideas as too dangerous to ignore, and so they convened a synod in the city of Dordrecht (also known as "Dort") in 1618–19. They invited voting representatives from Reformed churches in eight countries, including England. It was, therefore, an "international" gathering of proponents of the Reformed faith to determine whether Arminius's teaching was consistent with the Belgic Confession. The synod convened on November 13, and consisted of eighty-six voting members. They examined the five points advanced by the Remonstrants. Failing to reconcile these with God's Word, they unanimously rejected them. They then articulated the true teaching of Scripture in five chapters, which are known today as "the five points of Calvinism."

From the perspective of historical hindsight, it is well within the mark to say that the main issues under discussion at the Synod of Dort were those raised, expressed, and defended by Perkins two decades earlier. In this respect, we see his theological influence—as well as that of others—extending well beyond the shores of England to the development of Reformed theology in general. Perkins was committed to the Reformed doctrine of predestination because he was convinced that, if God's grace in predestination is contingent upon our faith and works, then we are ultimately the author of salvation, while God becomes nothing more than an impotent bystander. For Perkins, such a thing was inconceivable. He was untiring, therefore, in his defense of the Reformed doctrine—a defense that proved paradigmatic for centuries to come.

5

THE CHURCHMAN

During the reign of Bloody Mary, many Protestants were burned at the stake. These included Archbishop of Canterbury Thomas Cranmer, Bishops John Hooper, Nicholas Ridley, and Hugh Latimer, and preachers such as John Bradford and John Rogers. These men were accused of heresy, as Mary turned England back to Roman Catholicism. John Foxe records a particularly moving account of the martyrdom of Ridley and Latimer:

A lighted fagot was now laid at Dr. Ridley's feet, which caused Mr. Latimer to say: "Be of good cheer, Ridley, and play the man. We shall this day by God's grace light such a candle in England as, I trust, will never be put out."

When Dr. Ridley saw the fire flaming up towards him, he cried with a wonderful loud voice, "Lord, Lord, receive my spirit." Mr. Latimer, crying as vehemently on the other side, "O Father of heaven, receive my soul!" received the flame, as it were, embracing it. After he had stroked his face with his hands, and as it were, bathed them a little in the fire, he soon died (as it appears) with very little pain or none.

Well, dead they are, and the reward of this world they have already. What reward remains for them in heaven, the day of the Lord's glory, when he comes with His saints, shall declare.

During the same period, many more Protestants fled to the Continent. In 1554, the greatest number of these exiles lived in Frankfurt. They were united in their opposition to Mary, but that is where their agreement ended. They did not share a common view on the extent of the Reformation in England. Many supported the Prayer Book produced during Edward's reign, and they desired to work within the Church of England. But others dissented from the Prayer Book. These dissenters constituted the original group of English to arrive at Frankfurt. Having settled, they summoned John Knox from Geneva to be their pastor. Under Knox's pastoral oversight, they adopted a modified version of the Prayer Book, which abolished the use of priestly vestments, oral responses, and any other practice deemed inconsistent with the Reformed faith.

When Bishop John Hooper was burned at the stake in 1555, a new wave of exiles arrived at Frankfurt. They were led by Richard Cox, vice-chancellor of Oxford. On their first Sunday, they made it known that they desired "the face of an English church." From that moment, the congregation was divided between supporters of Knox and Cox. Within two weeks of his arrival, Cox had persuaded the civil magistrates that the Prayer Book was consistent with Reformed standards. He also exerted political pressure whereby the magistrates asked Knox to leave the city.

Before long, the Cox faction had control of the church, while most of Knox's followers departed for Geneva. There, Knox's followers adopted an order of discipline, prayer book, and liturgy designed by John Calvin.

These troubles at Frankfurt previewed a coming storm within the Church of England. The division between the "Prayer Book" faction (Cox) and "Bible" faction (Knox) was related in large part to the question of authority in the ordering of public worship. The Cox group appealed to established norms, whereas the Knox group appealed to Scriptural forms. When Mary died on November 17, 1558, Elizabeth was installed as the new monarch, and the Frankfurt division soon took center stage.

At the outset of her reign, one of Elizabeth's ministers summarized the nation's state of affairs as follows:

> The queen poor; the realm exhausted; the nobility decayed; good captains and soldiers waning; the people out of order; justice not executed; all things dear; excesses in meat, diet, and apparel; divisions among ourselves; war with France; the French king bestriding the realm, having one foot in Calais and the other in Scotland; steadfast enemies, but no steadfast friends.

Given England's deplorable condition, Elizabeth's ministers urged caution and moderation. She listened. She was well aware of the fact that she had to deal with prevailing sensibilities at home; moreover, she had to take foreign interests into account. Simply put, she did not want to offend the Lutheran princes of Germany, or antagonize the Roman Catholic kings in the rest of Europe. For this reason, Elizabeth adopted what is known as a *via media* (middle way). Today, it is known as the Elizabethan

Settlement. It actually rested on two acts of parliament in 1559—the Act of Supremacy and the Act of Uniformity. The first restored the supremacy of the Church of England to the monarch, while the second enforced the new Prayer Book—a revised edition of Edward VI's prayer book.

The passing of these acts was never a foregone conclusion, owing to the fact that the Marian bishops still controlled the House of Lords. In an attempt to deal with the stalemate, Elizabeth summoned eight Catholics and eight Protestants to debate the following propositions:

> First, it is against the Word of God and the custom of the ancient church to use a tongue, unknown to the people, in common prayer and the administration of the sacraments. Second, every church has authority to appoint, take away, and change ceremonies and ecclesiastical rites, so long as they are edifying. Third, it cannot be proved by the Word of God that there is offered up in the mass a propitiatory sacrifice for the living and the dead.

After several days of debate, two of the Catholics (both bishops) were imprisoned for "disobedience to common authority." This served to weaken Catholic opposition in the House of Lords and, as a result, the Act of Supremacy and the Act of Uniformity were eventually passed. These acts introduced significant additions and omissions designed to further Elizabeth's policy of moderation. She maintained the form of church worship and government to which her people were accustomed. The congregation still bowed at the name of Jesus, and knelt during the reading of the litany. Clergy still dressed in their traditional habits. At the same time, however, she made necessary changes to appease Protestants. She ensured that an English translation of the Bible was placed in every church. Relics, images, and monuments were removed from churches. Prayers to the saints were abolished. Most significantly, the fourteen surviving bishops from Mary's reign were removed from office.

Four years later in 1563, the Church of England established the Thirty-Nine Articles of Religion. Parliament authorized these eight years later in 1571. The articles clearly placed the Church of England within the framework of ancient councils, historic creeds, and orthodox doctrines. They also espoused the teaching of the Protestant Reformation on Scripture, free will, justification, and good works. At the same time, they openly opposed Catholic dogmas such as purgatory and transubstantiation, and Catholic practices such as invoking the saints and adoring the Eucharist.

But not everyone was pleased with Elizabeth's *via media*. Obviously, Roman Catholics lamented the reversal of Mary's policies, while Protestants were split over the extent of the Reformation in England. This split reflected the old Frankfurt debate. Some were satisfied with the Elizabeth Settlement, but others were discouraged with the state of the church, and desired to remove all perceived remnants of Roman Catholicism. Some of them also desired to reform the church's government on the basis of Presbyterianism. These men encompassed a broad spectrum of opinion, yet all shared one common denominator—dissatisfaction with the extent of the Reformation. As one historian notes:

> The term "Puritan" became current during the 1560s as a nickname for Protestants who, dissatisfied with

the Elizabethan Settlement of the church by the Act of Uniformity of 1559, would have subscribed to the contention of the Admonition to Parliament of 1572 that "we in England are so far off, from having a church rightly reformed, according to the prescript of God's Word, that as yet we are not come to the outward face of the same."

The authors of the Admonition to Parliament, John Field and Thomas Wilcox, viewed the Prayer Book as "imperfect ... culled and picked out of the popish dunghill." They wanted to see the English church organized on the basis of Scripture alone. This Puritan movement continued unabated until John Whitgift became Archbishop of Canterbury in 1583. He made the suppression of Puritanism one of his chief priorities. He produced six articles to which all clergy were required to assent. They included strict adherence to the Thirty-Nine Articles of Religion and the Prayer Book. As a result of his strict policy, over two hundred ministers were suspended. "The name Puritan," penned Whitgift, "is very aptly given to these men, not because they are pure, but because they think themselves to be more pure than others."

As for Perkins, he never openly allied himself with these Puritans. He was particularly dismissive of those who called for separation from the Church of England. "No man," says he, "ought to sever himself from the Church of England because of some wants therein. We have the true doctrine of Christ preached among us by God's blessing, and though there are corruptions in manners among us, and though some could justly find fault with our doctrine, yet so long as we hold Christ, no man ought to sever himself from our church."

That being said, Perkins did occasionally express his dissatisfaction over the condition of the church. On January 19, 1587, he appeared before the Vice-Chancellor at Cambridge to give an account for a sermon (preached in the college chapel), in which he allegedly railed against "superstitious" and "antichristian" practices in the church. Among other things, he objected to kneeling upon receiving the sacrament, he objected to the minister self-administering the bread and wine as opposed to receiving it from another, and he objected to facing east toward the cross while receiving the Lord's Supper.

As he stood before the Vice-Chancellor, Perkins denied some of the charges while modifying several of his comments. For starters, he denied having rejected the practice of kneeling while receiving the sacrament. He had simply suggested that sitting was more appropriate based on the fact that Christ sat while administering the Supper. He added, "In things indifferent we must go as far as we can from idolatry." As for self-administering the bread and wine, he argued that in the context of the college chapel it was better to receive the elements from another. Since there were thirteen ministers present at the Supper, he thought it was appropriate to administer the elements to one another. "By this means," says he, "the minister not only receives the sacrament, but also receives approbation from his brother that he is a worthy receiver." Finally, Perkins defended his objection to turning east to face the cross: "I marvel why the cross still stands in the window, and why we turn ourselves toward the end of the chapel at the end of the first and second lesson." For Perkins, this practice had Rome written all over it.

Perkins concluded his defense by openly admitting:

"I might have spoken at a better and more convenient time." He subsequently informed a gathering in the college chapel that he had not intended to disquiet the university. After this brush with the authorities, it appears that he intentionally steered clear of such controversies.

In 1591, Perkins faced a struggle of a slightly different nature. He appeared in the Star Chamber as a witness for the prosecution in a trial of several Puritan ministers. He was examined about a conference he had attended in 1589 at St. John's College, Cambridge. Laurence Chaderton, the master of Emmanuel College at the time, and Thomas Cartwright, a former fellow of Trinity College and Lady Margaret Professor of Divinity, had also been in attendance. The theme of the conference was a book of discipline, arguing for the merits of a Presbyterian form of church government over an Episcopal form of church government.

At the trial, Perkins acknowledged that he was present for a discussion of "whether the said book of discipline was agreeable to the Word of God." He confirmed the presence of several of the defendants in the case, but refused to divulge any additional names of those who had been present. Asked if participants had discussed how to advance the Presbyterian cause, Perkins stated that he did not know "that any ministers did at any time meet at any place for the purpose" of discussing or debating "how the said discipline might be advanced or practiced."

Perkins's evasive testimony suggests something of a struggle in his mind. On the one hand, he likely agreed with some of the proposed innovations regarding church worship and government. On the other hand, he was not prepared to be contentious about such things. Perkins viewed himself as a loyal member of the Church of England. When it came to those things that were secondary issues in his estimation, his first priority remained the peace of the church. Touching the debates about church government, he penned: "We all agree in the substance of the order, confessing that there must be preaching of the Word, administration of the sacraments according to their institution, and the use of the power of the keys in admonitions, suspensions, and excommunications. The difference between us only touches the persons, and the manner of putting this government in execution."

While unwavering in his loyalty to the Church of England, Perkins was at the same time deeply concerned about its spiritual condition. Writing in the 1590s, he remarked, "We are not now what we were twenty or thirty years ago." He blamed the church's woeful spiritual condition on the fact that "the remainders of popery still stick in the minds of most people, and they think that to serve God is nothing more than to deal fairly with others and babble a few words morning and evening at home or in the church." As far as Perkins was concerned, the church still suffered the ill-effects of the Roman Catholic dogma of implicit faith. That is to say, most people still assumed that as long as they accepted "some necessary points of religion" they were good Christians. Yet, according to one report, these same people "love a pot of ale better than a pulpit and a corn-rick better than a church door; who, coming to the divine service more for fashion than devotion, are content to sing a psalm or slumber during a sermon."

This was one of the chief reasons why Perkins was not so

concerned about the external forms of the church. Instead of focusing his attention on church polity, he was primarily concerned with addressing pastoral inadequacies, spiritual deficiencies, and widespread ignorance within the church. In an early work, *The Foundation of Christian Religion*, published in 1590, Perkins addressed his readers as follows: "you lead your lives in great ignorance, as may appear by your common opinions." These include:

> That God is served by the rehearsing of the Ten Commandments, the Lord's Prayer, and the Creed.

> That it was a good world under the old religion, because all things were cheap.

> That a man may swear by the mass because it is nothing now, and by our Lady because she has departed the country.

> That if a man remembers to say his prayers in the morning (even though he never understands them), he has blessed himself for the whole day.

For Perkins, these "opinions" betrayed the ignorance still so prevalent among his fellow countrymen. For this reason, he understood the church's most pressing need not in terms of ecclesiastical innovation, but theological instruction. Perkins viewed the church as being sound in its official doctrine and worship, yet woefully hampered on account of inadequate teaching. He understood his calling in terms of filling this void, thereby bringing others to a better understanding of the faith.

6

THE FELLOW

The original charter of Christ's College, issued in 1505, provided for sixty people to live on the foundation of the college: one master, twelve fellows, and forty-seven scholars. The fellows were elected for an indefinite period of time, and were responsible for preaching as well as conducting lectures. Paying students were given the services of tutors, who acted as "guides to learning as well as guardians of finances, morals, and manners." Since tutors and students often shared the same room, direct and indirect teaching was constant. This close relationship meant that a student's education was often life-changing.

As a fellow and tutor, Perkins's influence was immeasurable. From 1584 to 1595, he was the chief attraction at Christ's College. Samuel Ward, a former student, reflected in his diary: "O, my thankfulness for God's benefits ... He selected me from among my brethren to come to Cambridge ... to this college, and during Mr. Perkins's time." In addition to tutoring, Perkins catechized students at Corpus Christi College on Thursday afternoons. He also worked as an adviser on Sunday afternoons, counseling the spiritually distressed. In these various roles, he left an indelible mark on a generation of young men, including Richard Sibbes, John Cotton, John Preston, and William Ames. In the preface to one of his own works, Ames remarks:

> I gladly call to mind the time, when being young, I heard worthy Mr. Perkins so preach in a great assembly of students that he instructed them soundly in the truth, stirred them up effectually to seek after godliness, made them fit for the kingdom of God, and by his own example showed them what things they should chiefly pursue, so that they might promote the power of true religion unto God's glory and others' salvation.

During his time at Cambridge, Perkins's reputation was unrivalled. When Thomas Goodwin enrolled at the university in 1613, a full ten years after Perkins's death, he could write, "The town was then filled with the discourse of the power of Mr. Perkins's ministry, still fresh in most men's memories." Perkins's popularity stemmed in part from his stature as an eminent scholar. Naturally, the depth and breadth of his learning appealed to students. From all personal accounts, he was affable and approachable. These features undoubtedly contributed to his appeal as well. But there was something more. In a word, Perkins presented a pastoral ideal that appealed to undergraduates preparing for the ministry. That is to say, they heard something worth assimilating in his teaching and something worth emulating in his example. Perkins's pastoral ideal arose out of four heart-felt concerns.

For starters, Perkins was concerned not only about the lack of preachers in the Church of England (there were only 7,000 ordained ministers for 9,000 livings in the 1580s), but about the lack of capable preachers. Prayer Book services, homilies, and catechisms introduced Protestant teaching to the people; however, these things did not lead them to deeper devotion. The average person was content with the minimum required of religious observance. In 1593, Perkins complained, "When popery was first banished from our land, there was more knowledge than there is now. The more it is preached, the more ignorant and hardened people become. We can preach until our lungs fly out, yet men are no more moved than stones." While recognizing the depravity of the human heart, Perkins believed that the state of the church was explained by the lack of capable pastors: "When we see a people without knowledge and without good guides or teachers, or when we see one stand up in the congregation unable to teach, here is a matter for mourning." Acknowledging this, he made the training of young men for ministry a chief priority.

Closely related to the above, Perkins was concerned about the prevalence of false teachers within the church: Arians, Donatists, Papists, Libertines, Anabaptists—to name but a few. He was aware of Christ's warning to beware of those who infiltrate the church in "sheep's clothing," but are really "ravenous wolves" (Matthew 7:15). According to Perkins, these false teachers maintain "some error that overturns true faith and religion." He adds, "By their damnable doctrine they seek to poison and corrupt the souls of simple men." Pastors must, therefore, "beware" of false teachers by laboring "to maintain the faith." Perkins encouraged pastors to do so by: remembering that God had restored "true religion" to England; esteeming those men who were the means by which God restored "pure religion"; searching and studying "the Holy Scriptures"; praying to God "for illumination"; and keeping "a good conscience."

For Perkins, the main difficulty in dealing with these "false prophets" is their duplicity—they appear "in sheep's clothing" (Matthew 7:15). To remedy this, he carefully highlighted the marks of a true prophet. For starters, a true prophet "teaches and preaches in the name of God," but a false prophet comes in his own name. Next, a true prophet handles Scripture in a "right and wholesome" manner, but a false prophet does not—his doctrine "is contrary to the wholesome doctrine of holy Scriptures." Finally, a true prophet "seeks God's glory," but a false prophet "seeks not God's glory, but his own."

Perkins's third concern as he surveyed the Church of England was the lack of adequate training available for pastors. The bachelor degree was void of any formal theological education; moreover, it provided no training in how to preach or provide pastoral care. The widespread assumption was that any educated man could figure out how to preach, counsel the distressed, comfort the sick, encourage the dying, and challenge the wayward. Perkins was most certainly not opposed to the university curriculum; on the contrary, he embraced it as a vital component in pastoral preparation. He believed the study of Scripture required knowledge of the arts, because these lead pastors into a deeper understanding of Scripture. But Perkins recognized that something more was needed at the university level. He believed that it was necessary to set out ministerial duties in detail.

Lastly, Perkins was concerned about the popular style of preaching. He believed that it was weighed down with human learning, thus rendering it ineffective. A pastor's aim should not be the demonstration of his skill, but the demonstration of God's power. Such power is evident when people judge that the Holy Spirit is speaking through the preacher's words and gestures. This is one of the reasons why a preacher's words must be plain. "A strange word hinders the understanding of those things that are spoken," explains Perkins. "It draws the mind away from the purpose to some other matter." Closely related to this, Perkins perceived that far too many preachers were overly concerned with the "trimmings" of their sermons and, therefore, unable to convey Christ in a living way to their people. It was essential, for Perkins, that a preacher possess not only "the knowledge of divine things flowing in his brain but engraved on his heart and printed in his soul by the spiritual finger of God." A preacher should proclaim God's Word in such a way that a man's "conscience is so convinced, his secret faults so disclosed, and his very heart so ripped up, that he will say, 'Certainly God speaks in this man.'"

Out of these concerns over the state of pastoral ministry in the Church of England arose Perkins's *The Art of Prophesying.* In this treatise, he laid out "the sacred and only method of preaching" in four steps. The first is "to read the text distinctly out of the canonical Scriptures." At this point, Perkins's conviction regarding the authority and sufficiency of Scripture is clearly evident. He believed in the "canonical" Scriptures, consisting of the thirty-nine books of the Old Testament and the twenty-seven books of the New Testament. These, for Perkins, constitute the "wisdom of God concerning the truth." As such, they alone form the substance of preaching.

Closely related to this, Perkins condemned those who trusted in "revelations of the Spirit" while denigrating "the study of the Scriptures." He was adamant that any pretended experience of the Holy Spirit divorced from the Word was suspect. "Let no man think I give the least allowance to Anabaptist fancies and revelations, which are nothing but their dreams or the devil's illusions." Perkins was equally adamant that the Holy Spirit "only works upon the foundation of the Word." In other words, the nature of the Holy Spirit's work in the authors of Scripture was unique. He now illuminates what He then inspired. The guidance of the Holy Spirit, therefore, is inseparable from the Word of God. This means that the pastor's task is simply to expound what the Holy Spirit has revealed in Scripture.

The second step in preaching is "to give the sense and understanding" of the text. This is known as interpretation: "the opening of the words and sentences of the Scripture, so that one entire and natural sense may appear." Perkins's process was straightforward. It begins with reading Scripture systematically, beginning with Romans, John, and Psalms, then extending to the prophets (primarily Isaiah) and the historical books. As for specific rules of interpretation, Perkins encouraged students to consider the literary style and structure of the text, then open up "words and sentences." He also encouraged students to ask questions of each text. How does it relate to the principal themes of Scripture? What is its context: author, audience, and purpose? What other passages of Scripture shed light on it?

The third step in preaching is "to collect a few and profitable points of doctrine." Perkins described this as "the right dividing of the Word." It simply involves deducing the point of a passage: theologically and practically.

The fourth and final step in preaching is "to apply the doctrines rightly collected to the life and manners of men in a simple and plain speech." This is where Perkins excelled, carefully dividing his audience into seven categories:

1 *Ignorant and unteachable unbelievers.* They need to be prepared to receive the doctrine of the Word by clear, reasonable teaching as well as by reproof and pricking of their consciences.

2 *Ignorant but teachable unbelievers.* Perkins says these must be catechized in the foundational doctrines of the Christian religion. He recommends his book written for that purpose, *Foundations of the Christian Religion,* which covers the subjects of repentance, faith, the sacraments, the application of the Word, the resurrection, and the last judgment.

3 *Those who have some knowledge but remain unhumbled.* To them the preacher must especially proclaim the law to stir within them sorrow and repentance for sin, followed by the preaching of the gospel.

4 *The humbled.* The preacher must not give comfort to such people too soon, but must first determine whether their humility results from God's saving work

rooted in faith or from mere common conviction. To the partly humbled who are not yet stripped of their righteousness, Perkins says that the law must be propounded yet more, albeit tempered with the gospel, so that "being terrified with their sins, and with the meditation of God's judgment, they may together at the same instant receive solace by the gospel." To the fully humbled, "the doctrine of faith and repentance, and the comforts of the gospel ought to be proclaimed and tendered."

5 *Those who believe.* Believers need to be taught the key doctrines of justification, sanctification, and perseverance, along with the law as the rule of conduct rather than its sting and curse. "Before faith, the law with the curse is to be preached; after conversion, the law without the curse," Perkins writes.

6 *Those who are fallen, either in faith or in practice.* Those who backslide in faith fall in knowledge or in apprehending Christ. If they fall in knowledge, they are to be instructed in the particular doctrine from which they have erred. If they fail to apprehend Christ, they should examine themselves by the marks of grace, then fly to Christ as the remedy of the gospel. Those who fall in practice are those who fall into some sinful behavior. They need to be brought to repentance by the preaching of the law and the gospel.

7 *A mixed group.* These people are not easy to categorize because they are a combination of the first six kinds of listeners. Much wisdom is needed to know how much law and how much gospel to bring to them.

Perkins sought to apply doctrines to each of these groups

by way of correction, admonition, and exhortation. "Thus any place of Scripture ought to be handled," he said, and doctrines "fitly applied to the present condition of the church."

Perkins was committed to this very simple method of preaching (interpretation of text, explanation of doctrines, and application of doctrines) because he believed that it was the best way to convince the judgment and embrace the affections, thereby bringing the mind into vital contact with the meaning of Scripture. Furthermore, he believed that this method of preaching would go a long way to address many of the prevailing inadequacies within the church.

This pastoral ideal accounts for much of Perkins's appeal at Cambridge. He spoke directly to the prevailing conditions within the church and to the most pressing needs of those preparing for ministry. His insights became the standard for a generation of young men, thereby shaping the pulpit and pew well into the next century.

7

THE PREACHER

After his ordination to the ministry, Perkins began to preach on Sundays to the prisoners at Cambridge Castle. Apparently, he was able to pronounce "the word *damn* with such an emphasis as it left a doleful echo in his auditors' ears a good while after." Moreover, he applied "the terrors of the law so directly to the consciences of his hearers that their hearts would often sink under conviction." By all accounts, he was God's chosen instrument in bringing salvation to many.

On one occasion, Perkins confronted a condemned prisoner who was climbing the gallows, looking "half-dead." Perkins reportedly said to the man: "What is the matter with you? Are you afraid of death?" The prisoner confessed that he was less afraid of death than of what would follow. Perkins responded, "Come down again man, and you will see what God's grace will do to strengthen you." The prisoner complied. They knelt together, and Perkins offered "such an effectual prayer in confession of sins as made the poor prisoner burst out into abundance of tears." Convinced the prisoner was brought "low enough, even to hell's gates," Perkins showed him the freeness of the gospel. The prisoner's eyes were opened "to see how the black lines of all his sins were crossed and cancelled with the red lines of his crucified Savior's precious blood; so graciously applying it to his wounded conscience as made him break out into new showers of tears for joy of the inward consolation which he found." The prisoner climbed cheerfully up the ladder, testified of salvation in Christ's blood, and bore his death with patience, "as if he actually saw himself delivered from the hell which he feared before, and heaven opened for the receiving of his soul, to the great rejoicing of the beholders."

Perkins's preaching attracted people from the town and university. There were a number of reasons for this. To begin with, he was convinced of the centrality of preaching in pastoral ministry because he viewed it as the chief means by which God imparts grace to His people. Given his theology of preaching, it is no surprise that he gave himself wholeheartedly to it. He adapted his scholastic learning to the needs of his people because he was determined to preach sermons that appealed to every listener. He was committed to ensuring that his preaching was clear, simple, and direct. As one biographer observes, "His sermons were not so plain but that the piously learned did admire them, nor so learned but that the plain did understand them."

Another factor contributing to Perkins's popularity was his style of preaching. He was opposed to "memorizing" sermons because he believed it quenched liberty in preaching. "He who fears to stumble at one word," says he, "confounds his own memory." Furthermore, he was convinced that memorization hinders "pronunciation, action, and the holy motions of the affections, because the mind is wholly occupied" with its efforts to remember. Perkins's approach was straightforward. As he prepared each sermon, he studied and prepared until he was familiar with the content of his message. Then, he developed a clear sermon outline accompanied by arguments and illustrations. He felt that this approach allowed for liberty in expression. This liberty was facilitated by Perkins's use of voice and body. His voice was moderate when delivering doctrine, yet fervent when applying God's truth to the heart. His bodily gestures conveyed gravity while allowing for the motions of his arms, hands, and eyes to express "the godly affections of the heart."

The third reason for Perkins's popularity as a preacher was his personal godliness. In the words of one contemporary, "he lived his sermons, and as his preaching was a comment on his text, so his practice was a comment on his preaching." As far as Perkins was concerned, God's grace must be evident in a preacher. Such grace includes a good conscience before God and man, and an inward feeling of God's truth. It also includes the fear of God, love for people, constancy in life, and temperance in conduct. In Perkins's estimation, holiness in a preacher is absolutely necessary, because God "abhors the combination of godly speech and an ungodly life." Equally important, Perkins realized that "people do not see the ministry but the person of the minister" and, for this reason, there must be consistency between a pastor's words and walk. By all accounts, Perkins adhered to this, and practiced what he preached.

The fourth, and perhaps most important, reason for

Perkins's popularity as a preacher was his ability to apply God's Word. One auditor reported that each of Perkins's sermons "seemed all law and all gospel, all cordials and all corrosives, as the different necessities of people apprehended it." Perkins's ability to apply God's Word flowed directly from his understanding of how God works faith in the heart.

For starters, God "prepares the heart that it may be acceptable of faith." He does so by "humbling and softening" it through the law. Recognizing this, Perkins gave a lot of attention in his sermons to probing his auditors' hearts and lives "by the commandments of the law." He believed that the tenth commandment was particularly effective in this regard. After all, it "was the means of Paul's conversion." In Romans 7:7, Paul writes, "What shall we say then? Is the law sin? God forbid. Nay, I had not known sin, but by the law: for I had not known lust, except the law had said, 'Thou shalt not covet.'" Through this commandment, Paul realized that sin is not primarily concerned with deeds, but desires. In addition, he recognized that his desires were as damnable as his deeds. Up until that moment, he knew the law theoretically, but he did not know it experientially. But Paul came to know his sin by the Holy Spirit's work through the law. In Perkins's words, the tenth commandment "ransacked" Paul's heart.

When we see our sin like this, we experience "a pain and pricking in the heart arising from the feeling of the displeasure of God." Perkins equated this "pain and pricking" with the "spirit of bondage" mentioned in Romans 8:15. "This sorrow is called the 'spirit of bondage to fear,'" explains Perkins, "because when a man sees his sin, he also sees the curse of the law, and he sees himself in bondage under Satan, hell, death, and damnation. At this most terrible sight, his heart is smitten with fear and trembling." This sorrow, in turn, creates a "holy desperation ... when a man is out of all hope of attaining salvation by any of his own strength or goodness." This was what Perkins aimed at in his preaching. He sought to apply the law in such a way as to bring people to cry, "What shall we do?" (Acts 2:37).

Having thus prepared the heart by "humbling and softening," God then "causes faith by little and little to spring and breed in the heart." He does this by stirring us to "ponder most diligently the great mercy of God offered in Christ." As a result, we feel and acknowledge our "need of Christ," and cry with the poor publican, "God be merciful to me a sinner!" After this, "a lively assurance of the forgiveness of sin" arises in the heart. For a "better understanding" of this entire process, Perkins appealed to the fact "that a sinner is often compared to a sick man in the Scriptures." His point is that what disease is to the body sin is to the soul; moreover, the method of curing disease points to the method of curing sin. When we are convinced that we suffer from a disease, we immediately call for the doctor. When the doctor arrives, we yield ourselves to his counsel, and willingly accept whatever remedy he prescribes. The same is true when it comes to faith in Christ. When we are absolutely convinced of our need, we submit to His cure.

Perkins's point is that we must perceive our real need, in order to come to Christ. We must be "thirsty" before we will drink of Christ; we must be "hungry" before we will feed on Christ; we must be "weary and heavy-laden" before we will rest in Christ (Matthew 11:28–30); we must be like a "battered reed" (i.e., easy to break off) and a "smoldering wick" (i.e., easy to put out) before we will turn to Christ (Matthew 12:20). For Perkins, there must be humiliation for sin before there will ever be faith in Christ.

These, then, are the two steps by which God works faith in the heart: first, He prepares the heart for faith by "humbling and softening" it; and, second, He causes faith to breed "little by little" in the heart. For Perkins, the means by which God accomplishes this is the preaching of His Word: "The only ordinary means to attain faith is by the Word preached. It must be heard, remembered, practiced, and continually hid in the heart." From this conviction flowed Perkins's commitment, not only to preaching, but to preaching in a searching manner, applying God's Word at every turn.

Perkins's approach is evident in his interpretation of Christ's words in Matthew 5:13–16. Here, Christ begins by describing ministers as "salt," in order to teach them how to "dispense" God's Word. In short, they must seek to express the properties of salt. Perkins explains, "The properties of salt applied to raw flesh or fresh wounds are principally three. First, it bites and frets, being of nature hot and dry. Second, it makes meats savoury to our taste. Third, it preserves meat from rotting by drawing out superfluous moisture." The pastor's application of God's Word to people's hearts must have the same three-fold effect. It must bite: "The law must be applied to rip up men's hearts, to make them see their sins. It must fret and bite them, to cause them to renounce themselves." It must season: "The gospel must be preached, so that men feel their corruption like rottenness in their souls, and are seasoned with grace and thereby reconciled to God." It must preserve: "Both the law and the gospel must be continually dispensed, so that sin and corruption might be mortified and consumed daily in heart and life."

In these verses, Christ then describes ministers as "light." To avoid any misunderstanding of what this means, Perkins explains that there are two kinds of light: "original" (the cause of light); and "reflected" (that light which is received from another). In the context, Christ is the "original" light, while His ministers are the "reflected" light. Ministers reflect Christ's light in their lives and pulpits, meaning they perform good works for people to see, and they preach God's Word for people to hear.

In terms of performing good works, Perkins maintained that the "similitude" of light points to the "holiness" of the minister's life. This leads him to a discussion of the threefold use of good works. First, they have a God-ward function, in that they are a means whereby we express our reverence for, obedience of, and thankfulness to God. Second, they have a self-ward function, in that they serve as "testimonies" of the reality of our faith, and as "pledges" of our election, justification, sanctification, and glorification. In short, "they serve to make us answerable to our holy calling, for everyone who professes the gospel is called to be a member of Christ, and a new creature, whose duty is to bring forth good works." Third, they have a man-ward function, in that they serve to "win some unto God, and keep others in the obedience of the truth, and prevent offences, whereby many are drawn back."

In terms of preaching God's Word, Perkins believed the "similitude" of light is significant for two reasons. First, it "shows the right use of the ministry of the Word. The whole world lies in darkness, that is, in ignorance under sin, and so subject to damnation by nature. Now God has ordained the ministry of the Word to be a light, whereby this ignorance may be expelled, and people brought to the knowledge of their sins and of the way that leads to life." Second, it "shows how God's Word is to be handled, namely, so that it is a light to men's minds and consciences to make them see their sins and great misery, and then to see the remedy for that misery, which is Jesus Christ."

At this point, it is important to note that Perkins is not suggesting that there is an inherent power in preaching. He is aware that many people hear the preaching of God's Word without ever responding in faith and repentance. It is the Holy Spirit's work to illumine the mind and soften the heart, so that people receive God's Word. When He ministers in this fashion, people discern that what they are hearing "is in truth, the word of God" and they consequently embrace it with their heart (1 Thessalonians 2:13). For Perkins, this sovereign work of the Holy Spirit is absolutely necessary, because sin has such power over man that he is unwilling to respond to the preaching of the gospel (John 6:44, 65).

The general call is Christ's voice in the proclamation of His Word by the preacher; it is heard with the ear. But the effectual call is Christ's voice in the application of His Word by the Holy Spirit; it is heard with the soul. When God calls effectually, says Perkins, "the eyes of the mind are enlightened, the heart and ears opened, so that a man might see, hear, and understand the preaching of the Word of God." Perkins elaborates on the nature of this call by pointing to three "means." The first is "the saving hearing of the Word of God" whereby we hear the preaching of God's Word. The second is "the mollifying of the heart" whereby the Holy Spirit softens the heart, so that it is "fit to receive God's saving grace offered unto it." The third is "faith," which Perkins describes as "a miraculous and supernatural faculty of the heart." By the operation of the Holy Spirit, the heart "apprehends" and "receives" Christ.

In all this, Perkins clearly echoes John Calvin's concept of the "sacramental Word." "So then faith cometh by hearing, and hearing by the word of God," says the apostle Paul in Romans 10:17. Commenting on this verse, Calvin remarks, "This is a remarkable passage with regard to the efficacy of preaching, for Paul testifies that by it faith is produced... When it pleases the Lord to work, it becomes the instrument of His power."

Perkins embraced this paradigm wholeheartedly. In his preaching, he was determined to apply God's Word to man's heart because this was the vehicle by which the Holy Spirit exercised His power in the conversion of sinners. While in his final year of undergraduate study at Cambridge, John Cotton rejoiced inwardly when he heard the bells toll for Perkins's funeral. The cause of his secret delight was his deep-seated resentment towards Perkins for his disturbing sermons, which had destroyed his self-confidence and shredded his self-righteousness. But he finally surrendered to Christ several years later through the ministry of Richard Sibbes. By his own admission, it was the Holy Spirit working through Perkins's preaching that had prepared his heart.

8

The Pastor

When people turned to Perkins for spiritual counsel, they soon discovered a shepherd's heart. By all accounts, he was a skilled spiritual advisor, who excelled at adapting the wisdom of Scripture to every conceivable issue. This made him extremely popular, especially given the fact that English Protestants had very little literature that offered any insight on dealing with the problems of daily living. Perkins's writing and teaching, therefore, filled a gaping void. His pastoral counsel addressed the innumerable struggles that trouble Christians on their journey homeward.

One of the most significant of these struggles is related to our use of natural delights. How should we approach food, sleep, wealth, recreation, entertainment, etc.? What is permissible? Is there a line between enjoyment and indulgence? Underpinning Perkins's counsel was his concept of moderation, which he defined as a "virtue" that keeps "appetite or lust" in check. This virtue arises when the soul's affections are "tempered and allayed with the fear of God."

What are the affections? According to Perkins, they are the soul's inclination to a particular object. The soul loves whatever it perceives as good and, therefore, is inclined toward it. This inclination is expressed in desire (when the object is absent) and delight (when the object is present). Conversely, the soul hates whatever it perceives as evil and, therefore, is inclined away from it. This inclination is manifested in fear (when the object is absent) and sorrow (when the object is present).

For Perkins, it is important to understand how these affections operate before and after Adam's fall in the Garden of Eden. Prior to his fall, Adam's love was set on God and, consequently, his affections were well-directed. In a word, Adam was inclined to God. When he fell into sin, however, the object of his love changed. His love was no longer set on God, but self. That has been the condition of Adam's descendants ever since. It is known as the *flesh*.

In a state of regeneration, the Holy Spirit renews our love for God. As a result, our affections are "sanctified"—moved and inclined to that which is good, namely, God. For Perkins, this redirecting of our affections awaits perfection in the future, and it ushers in a great conflict between the flesh and the Spirit at present. For this reason, our daily duty is to make sure our affections are "tempered and allayed with the fear of God."

What is the fear of God? At the outset, it is extremely important to observe that Perkins distinguished between two kinds of fear: ungodly and godly. The first is the result of viewing God as a potential source of harm. It causes people to take steps to minimize the perceived threat, while remaining steadfast in their sin. For Perkins, this ungodly fear occurs "when a man only fears the punishment, and not the offence of God, or at least the punishment more than the offence." In marked contrast, godly fear is the result of viewing God as the greatest good. This may include a fear of God's wrath, but it is not limited to this; on the contrary, it focuses on God's majesty. Perkins affirmed that this fear is synonymous with fearing God's name—the fullest revelation of His glory. It is a fear that grips the affections, thereby making a divide between sin and the soul. In other words, it is a fear that manifests itself in the pursuit of holiness.

It is this fear that must temper our affections, especially as they relate to natural delights. As a result of the fall and our consequent alienation from God, we are tempted to pursue natural delights as our happiness. Consequently, they easily become idols, which we crave immoderately and abuse unthinkingly. When, however, the fear of God "tempers" and "allays" our affections, the result is moderation in our use of natural delights.

Perkins was no ascetic. He had no problem with recreation, food, music, sleep, etc. He remarks, "We may use these gifts of God not sparingly for mere necessity to satisfy our hunger and quench our thirst, but freely and liberally for Christian delight and pleasure. This is that liberty, which God has granted to all believers." The way to holiness, therefore, is not found in abstaining from God's good gifts, but in carefully enjoying them. We must not over-value natural delights according to our sinful inclinations; rather, we must moderate our use of them according to the fear of God. In his many directions governing the use of natural delights, Perkin's chief concern is that we put God before self, thereby avoiding idolatry. He encourages us to enjoy natural delights, echoing the words of the apostle Paul: "Whether therefore ye eat, or drink, or whatsoever ye do, do all to the glory of God" (1 Corinthians 10:31). The issue is not food, drink, or any other delight. They are good because God has ordained them. The issue is abuse, whereby we seek satisfaction in these things apart from God. We must moderate such inordinate desire. We do so when we enjoy natural delights in an attitude of thanksgiving, according to God's design.

A second struggle, frequently addressed by Perkins, is connected to our "calling" in this world. What qualifies as lawful employment? What is my responsibility at work? What is my role as a husband or wife? His pastoral insights on these and other related subjects are presented in *A Treatise of the Vocations*. His chief concern in writing was that "few men rightly know how to live and go on in their callings, so as to please God." To rectify this, he begins by distinguishing between two callings.

The first is "such as is of the essence and foundation of any society." Here, Perkins was thinking of ministers, magistrates, and most importantly members of a household. Perkins taught that the family was the basic unit of society; hence, the way to make godly parishes, godly nations, and godly kingdoms, was to make godly families. With that aim in view, he desired to instruct each family member in "the doctrine of true religion, so that they might know the true God, and walk in all His ways in doing righteousness."

In this connection, he placed particular emphasis on the

marital relationship. Perkins was married when he was thirty-seven years old, and evidently held the institution in high esteem. He affirmed that a husband's responsibilities included leading family worship, ensuring attendance at public worship, providing for his family, and keeping order within his home. A wife's responsibilities included advising her husband, maintaining her home, preparing meals, etc. Together, they exercised "power and authority over their children" in raising them according to the tenets of God's Word.

As for the marital bed, Perkins demonstrated little antipathy toward the body. Beginning in the second century, many allowed dualistic philosophies to influence their beliefs regarding sex. They held that lust taints all sexual activity. For many, this implied that virginity was superior to marriage. From this premise, the church of the medieval era acknowledged two reasons for marriage: the procreation of children and the avoidance of fornication. These notions remained prominent until the Reformers departed from the accepted tradition by adding a third reason for marriage, namely, mutual society. Perkins embraced this emphasis wholeheartedly, and also encouraged husbands and wives to delight in the marriage bed while guarding against inordinate passion. He emphasized Paul's teaching that a husband and wife were to give their bodies to each other, viewing sex in marriage as a "due benevolence" to each other.

The second kind of calling is "such as serves only for the good, happy, and quiet estate of society." In this regard, Perkins was thinking of employment. He called for honest and diligent labor in work, so as to serve the best interests of church and country. Foundational to Perkins's concept of work was his dismissal of the notion that the sacred referred to anything under the church's control whereas the secular referred to anything not under the church's control. All work is sacred in his eyes because it was a primary means by which people serve God. "We must," says Perkins, "consider the main end of our lives to serve God in the serving of others in the works of our callings." It would never have occurred to him that the two could be separated.

When speaking of vocations, Perkins appealed to Christ's declaration in Matthew 7:12, "Therefore all things whatsoever ye would that men should do to you, do ye even so to them." Perkins perceived two "things" in this commandment: "the thing to be ruled and ordered, namely our actions to other men"; and "the rule itself that must order all our sayings and doings towards others; namely, a desire for justice and equity." What motivates us to obey this commandment? The answer is our love for God, as Perkins explains:

> Our love to God must be shown in the practice of the duties of love, justice, and mercy towards men, for God is invisible, and it pleases Him to make Himself seen in our visible neighbor, requiring that our love for Him should be shown in our works of mercy, justice, and goodness, towards men. Men may flatter themselves, and say they love God, but if it is not shown in love for their neighbors, they deceive themselves. There is no love of God in them.

In his pastoral counsel, Perkins encouraged faithfulness in our callings whether at home or work. He warned that whoever "employs" his calling for himself, "seeking wholly his own, and not the common good" is guilty of abusing it. We must not fulfill our calling "slackly" or "carelessly," but as an occasion to glorify God. When we do, the works of our calling become "good works" in God's sight. For Perkins, this mindset radically altered the relationship between husband and wife, parent and child, employee and employer. In addition, it infused every calling—however insignificant in man's eyes—with worth and dignity. In this way, Perkins instructed Christians in how to cultivate godliness in their closest relationships and most familiar duties.

A third common struggle, which Perkins addressed regularly, arose from his role as a lecturer at Great St. Andrew's Church and fellow at Christ's College. He encountered Christians wrestling with a troubled conscience. In many instances, the cause of their distress was uncertainty concerning their relationship with God. Perkins addressed this predicament in many of his writings. One of his most popular was *The Whole Treatise of the Cases of Conscience*. It is based upon Isaiah 50:4, where the Servant of the Lord declares, "The Lord GOD hath given me the tongue of the learned, that I should know how to speak a word in season to him that is weary." Based on this verse, Perkins remarks, "It was one special duty of Christ's prophetical office to give comfort to the consciences of those who were distressed." Perkins believed that, by extension, it was also one of the chief duties of pastoral ministry.

According to one of his former students, William Ames, Perkins excelled at this aspect of pastoral ministry, for he knew how to "speak a word" to the weary by "untying and explaining cases of conscience." He did so through careful self-examination and faithful scriptural application. Like a skilled physician, Perkins would probe the heart, seeking to determine the ailment; then, he would apply the remedy.

In most cases, the remedy consisted of discerning God's will as revealed in Scripture. A thorough understanding of God's law was pivotal to this. When it comes to the Mosaic Law, Perkins was careful to make a threefold division. There is the "ceremonial" law: those laws that pertain to Israel's religion. There is also the "judicial" law: those laws that pertain to Israel's government. Finally, there is the "moral" law. According to Perkins, the moral law differs from the ceremonial and judicial laws, in that God did not give it exclusively to Israel, but to all humanity. It "was written in Adam's mind by the gift of creation, and the remnants of it are in every man by the light of nature." For Perkins, therefore, the ceremonial law was given exclusively to the Jews, the judicial law was given primarily to the Jews, but the moral law was given to everyone.

On the basis of Christ's claim in Matthew 5:18—"For verily I say unto you, Till heaven and earth pass, one jot or one tittle shall in no wise pass from the law, till all be fulfilled" (Matthew 5:18)—Perkins affirmed that the law is perpetual in three ways. As for the ceremonial law, it has been abrogated in that it no longer governs our worship; however, its "scope and substance" remains because it foreshadowed Christ and all His benefits. As for the judicial law, it has been abrogated because it was peculiar to the Jewish state, but it is perpetual in so far as it agrees with "common equity." As for the moral law, it "remains forever a rule of obedience to every child of God." We are not bound to obey it for our justification before God, but as a result of our justification before God.

In Perkins's opinion, therefore, the moral law is the unchanging "rule of obedience" for every follower of God. Much of his pastoral advice, as he sought to ease those in distress, was to lead them into a better understanding of God's will for them as revealed in His law.

A final area in which Perkins excelled in terms of his pastoral care was counseling those who were experiencing affliction. Despite the political and economic expansion of the Elizabethan era, not everyone prospered. The population grew from 2.98 million at the start of Elizabeth's reign to 4.1 million by 1600. The increased labor force meant that wages remained stagnant while prices increased. According to one estimate, twenty-five percent of families lived in poverty. Vagrancy was a problem across the land. Drought and famine were common occurrences. All of this was compounded by the absence of modern amenities, including medical care. In sum, Perkins ministered in a day in which affliction was the daily experience of many.

In counseling those in distress, Perkins emphasized the distinction between God's "general" and "special" providence. The first is "that which extends itself to the whole world and all things, even to the demons themselves." By this providence God "maintains the order" which He set in the creation, and He "preserves the life, substance, and being of all creatures." The second is "that which God shows and exercises towards His church and chosen people in gathering, guiding, and preserving them by His mighty power against the gates of hell." As for the relationship between the two, Christ governs His providential kingdom for the advancement of His spiritual kingdom. Two main tenets emerge from Perkins's view of God's providence.

The first is that God controls all things. This means that there is nothing that falls outside of the parameters of His control. Christ confirms this in Matthew 10:29, asking, "Are not two sparrows sold for a farthing? and one of them shall not fall on the ground without your Father." Based on these words, Perkins states, "God orders and directs all things to good ends. And it must be extended to the very least thing that is in heaven or earth, as to the sparrows." This necessarily implies that God controls all that befalls us in life—great and small.

The second tenet is that God controls all things for the good of His people. God is sovereign; therefore, His control is absolute. God is immutable; therefore, His will is certain. God is mighty; therefore, His power is limitless. God is most wise; therefore, His plan is perfect. God is incomprehensible; therefore, His providence is inscrutable. With this God before them, Christians—while not always understanding His ways—are certain that "all things work together for good" (Romans 8:28). This means that we are never in the grip of blind forces; rather, everything that happens to us is divinely planned.

For Perkins, the relationship between knowing God's providence and cultivating a "moderate care for worldly things" is of paramount importance. When we understand that God controls all things for our good, we can rest assured in the knowledge that He will provide for our needs in accordance with His infinite power and wisdom. We can be confident of His fatherly wise disposal in every circumstance. Perkins explains, "If there is a providence of

God over everything, then we must learn contentment of mind in every estate." For this reason, we must make every effort to familiarize ourselves with God's providence. "Such as profess the knowledge of the true God," says Perkins, "must better acquaint themselves with this providence and goodness of God, and labor to feel it in sickness and health, in poverty and wealth, in persecution and peace. When we can in some good measure do this, then our experience of divine providence will breed and bring forth contentment."

Perkins demonstrated a deep pastoral concern for others, and was determined to act as their spiritual guide by bringing God's Word to bear upon their lives. Such an approach reveals his unwavering conviction concerning the sufficiency of God's Word. He embraced it as the means through which God breaks a hard heart, humbles a proud heart, awakens a sleepy heart, encourages a troubled heart, enlightens a darkened heart, and regenerates a dead heart. It sustains in times of dark affliction, comforts in times of deep sorrow, strengthens in times of danger, and guides in times of confusion.

9

THE SABBATARIAN

In 1617, James I issued *The Book of Sports*, listing those sports and recreations permitted on Sundays. This declaration was an official attempt to resolve ongoing disputes concerning the observance of the Lord's Day. Among other things, archery, dancing, leaping, and vaulting were deemed "harmless recreation." Charles I, the next monarch, re-issued the declaration with slight modifications in 1633, but he took it a step further by requiring all ministers to read *The Book of Sports* publicly to their congregations. The opposition on the part of some ministers was vehement.

Why did these monarchs deem it necessary to meddle in such questions? In their own words, they were targeting "precise persons" who wanted to ban all recreational activity on Sundays. These "precise persons" were far from uniform in their opinions, but they did share a common denominator, namely, a particular understanding of the Lord's Day shaped by William Perkins. There were certainly other English theologians who expounded the subject, but

Perkins's views were foundational to the development of Sabbatarianism in England.

Perkins's understanding of the Lord's Day was based in large part on John Calvin's proposed third use of the law. Calvin asserted that the law has a "third and principal use" for those in "whose hearts the Spirit of God already lives and reigns—namely, to teach them to understand God's will more fully and arouse them to lives of obedience." Perkins agreed, and concluded that the moral law (as expressed in the Decalogue) was normative for all Christians. Naturally, this law included the fourth commandment: "Remember the sabbath day, to keep it holy" (Exodus 20:8). For Perkins, the conclusion was obvious: observing the Sabbath was as much an expression of love for God as observing any of the other commandments.

This view of the moral perpetuity of the Sabbath was the first distinct mark of Perkins's Sabbatarianism. He did not believe that God instituted the Sabbath at Sinai as part of Israel's religion, but back in the Garden of Eden before the fall of man. For Perkins, the implications were as follows: first, "there should be a day of rest on which man and beast might be refreshed after labor"; second, "this day should be sanctified, that is, set apart to the worship of God"; and third, "a seventh day should be sanctified to a holy rest, and that this holy rest should be observed on a seventh day."

The second mark of Perkins's Sabbatarianism was the change of the Sabbath from Saturday to Sunday. He provided a series of biblical proofs in support of this change. Most importantly, he argued that Christ's resurrection from the dead on the first day of the week, and

His subsequent appearances to His disciples on the first day of the week, marked the change of the Sabbath from Saturday to Sunday. His apostles confirmed this change by leading the New Testament to gather to worship on the first day of the week.

The third mark of Perkins's Sabbatarianism was a strict observance of the day. Faithful observance required a cessation from ordinary work, and a sanctification of the day to a holy life. "In the six days of the week," observes Perkins, "many men walk painfully in their calling, but when the Lord's Day comes, then every man takes license to do what he will." For Perkins, this was a direct violation of God's law.

Stepping back for a moment, we see how powerfully the motifs of creation, resurrection, and sanctification shaped the three marks of Perkins's Sabbatarianism. Coupled with this, we see Perkins's Trinitarian emphasis. As for the institution of the Sabbath, he believed that God the Father wrote it on the human heart at the time of creation along with all the other moral laws. Regarding the alteration of the Sabbath from Saturday to Sunday, he maintained that the apostles changed the day of worship to the first day of the week because of Christ's resurrection. Regarding the celebration of the Sabbath, he affirmed that its main purpose is to serve for the sanctification of God's people.

The Holy Spirit uses the Lord's Day to sanctify God's people, because this is the day on which they gather to commit themselves to the means of grace. Given his high regard for these means, it comes as little surprise that Perkins looked on the day itself as extremely important. He writes, "Whoever has not conscience on the Lord's Day to lift up his heart to heaven by prayer and hearing God's Word with meditation cannot possibly have any soundness in religion, nor his heart firmly set on heavenly things." This conviction led Perkins to label Sunday the market day of the soul—the day when the soul is nourished with products from the market of God's Word.

The first, and most important, of these means of grace is the preaching of God's Word. Perkins expected people to devote themselves to hearing from God on the Lord's Day; therefore, he prescribed directions, which he believed would help people glean all they could from their pastor's sermons. Before hearing God's Word, we must empty our hearts of evil frames. Perkins described this as "disburdening ourselves of all impediments, which may hinder the effectual hearing of the Word." Next, we must ask God "to give us a hearing ear." Equally important, we must approach the preaching of God's Word as if we were entering His very presence. Perkins believed that this would lead to sobriety—a great aid for listening attentively.

While hearing God's Word, we must strive to apply it to our lives. Whether it is the curses or commands of the law, or the comforts of the gospel, we must apply them by faith. In other words, we must listen to the preaching of God's Word as if God were speaking directly to us. "Every hearer," says Perkins, "must have care that the Word of God be rooted and grounded in his heart, like good seed in good ground." After hearing God's Word, our work is not finished. According to Perkins, we must "treasure" it in our hearts and "practice" it in our lives. In addition, we must meditate on what we have heard, examining ourselves in its light, and conforming our lives accordingly. Without this corresponding practice, listening to sermons is pointless.

The second means of grace is receiving the sacrament. Perkins did not believe that Christ was physically present in the bread and wine, and rejected the Roman Catholic doctrine of transubstantiation as a "fable." Christ's glorified body is in heaven; hence, there is an immeasurable distance between Christ and us. However, Christ comes down to us in the sacrament through the Holy Spirit. For Perkins, therefore, Christ's body and blood are really present in the bread and wine, but not locally, bodily, or substantially. This means that when we partake of the Lord's Supper, we consume Christ spiritually. Christ gives Himself in a spiritual manner, operating by His Spirit within us, so that "we might receive Christ with His benefits." This, in turn, imparts spiritual nourishment and draws us closer to Christ. In a word, the Holy Spirit "nourishes faith spiritually." We must, therefore, approach the sacrament in faith and repentance.

The third means of grace is praying. Perkins viewed ministers as "the mouth of the people to God." When they lead the congregation in prayer, people "must in fervent affection lift up their hearts to God, and give assent in their minds." This requires preparation. It is important for us to sever ourselves "from all creatures" in our "thoughts and desires," and present ourselves "before God with fear and reverence." How is this done? For starters, we must pursue whatever promotes prayer. This means meditating on our sins, needs, and mercies. This assists in prayer, because an appreciation of our sins leads to confession with shame and sorrow, an appreciation of our needs leads to petition with faith and fervency, and an appreciation of our mercies leads to thanksgiving with admiration and delight. This stirring of the heart enables us to pray with "zeal and diligence."

For Perkins, a diligent use of these means of grace is essential for sanctification, because God has appointed them as the vehicle by which the Holy Spirit works in us. We must, therefore, set aside the Lord's Day to pursue the means of grace. It is for this reason that, in Perkins's estimation, the Sabbath itself possessed sacramental significance. His reasoning was simple: if we partake of the means of grace on the Sabbath, then the Sabbath must be the primary means of those means of grace. "We must learn," therefore, "to sanctify the Sabbath of the Lord, or else we will never increase in faith, knowledge, or obedience."

10

THE PURITAN

Although Perkins preached about God's sovereign grace in salvation, he was particularly concerned about how this grace breaks through into our experience. He wanted to explain how we respond to God's sovereign grace; that is, how it impacts us so as to move us from initial faith to full assurance. At this point, Perkins's experimental piety steps to the fore. The term *experimental* comes from the Latin verb *experior*—"to know by experience." For Perkins, our experience of God's grace begins with humiliation. God "softens" our hearts by giving us a "sight of sin" arising from our knowledge of the law and a "sorrow for sin" arising from our knowledge of His displeasure. We recognize that we will never attain salvation by any "strength or goodness" of our own. Perceiving this, we acknowledge that we are without moral virtues adequate to commend ourselves to God, and that anything short of damnation is a mercy.

Having thereby softened our hearts, God now causes faith "to breed" in our hearts. When we are absolutely convinced of our need, we submit to His cure. God leads us to "ponder most diligently" His great mercy offered in Christ, and He brings us to acknowledge our "need of Christ" whereby we pray, "O God be merciful to me a sinner." Accompanying this faith is repentance, which Perkins defines as "a work of grace, arising of a godly sorrow whereby a man turns from all his sins to God." According to Perkins, God produces repentance by various "steps and degrees": the knowledge of the law of God, the nature of sin, the guilt of sin, and the judgment of God; the application of this knowledge to the heart by the Spirit of bondage; the consequent fear and sorrow; the knowledge of the gospel; the application of this knowledge to the heart by the Spirit of adoption; the consequent joy and sorrow; and the "turning of the mind whereby a man determines and resolves with himself to sin no more as he has done, but to live in newness of life."

From humiliation, faith, and repentance, our experience of God's sovereign grace moves to obedience. Perkins viewed the law as the point of contact between the covenant of works and the covenant of grace since obedience is fundamental to both covenants. He also asserted that the focus shifts between the two covenants from our obedience to Christ's obedience—the covenant of works having been fulfilled in the covenant of grace. For Perkins, therefore, we are free to obey the law in accordance with the new covenant. He affirmed that those who profess Christ's name seek to do the Father's will. He defined the Father's will in terms of two texts of Scripture. The first is John 6:40, where Christ declares, "And this is the will of him that sent me, that every one which seeth the Son, and believeth on him, may have everlasting life:

and I will raise him up at the last day." The second text is 1 Thessalonians 4:3–4, where the apostle Paul writes, "For this is the will of God, your sanctification, that ye should abstain from fornication: that every one of you should know how to possess his vessel in sanctification and honor." Based on these verses, Perkins maintained that "the doing of the Father's will" consists of three things: faith, repentance, and new obedience. Simply put, "new obedience" is the fruit of faith and repentance, whereby a man "endeavors to yield obedience to all God's commandments, from all the powers and parts both of his soul and his body." It is called *new* because "it is a renewing of that in man whereto he was perfectly enabled by creation."

For Perkins, this experience of God's sovereign grace in humiliation, faith, repentance, and obedience was absolutely essential. We must seek "the graces of God's children who are regenerate, even true faith, true repentance, and new obedience, and not rest in other gifts though they be most excellent." He was convinced that many people err at this very point because they satisfy themselves with "a general persuasion of God's mercy." But this "general persuasion" is not the same thing as genuine faith and repentance. It may produce "reformation of life," but it never produces "new obedience."

This discussion of "a general persuasion of God's mercy" naturally leads to Perkins's handling of the doctrine of assurance. By the late sixteenth century, the issue of assurance loomed large within the Church of England because of the growing tendency on the part of many to take God's saving grace for granted. Perkins particularly reacted to dead orthodoxy, which minimized the seriousness of sin and regarded mere assent to the truths of Scripture as sufficient for salvation. It thus became essential for him to distinguish between assurance and presumption. He was particularly troubled over the prevalence of civility within the professing church. "If we look into the general state of our people," says he, "we will see that religion is professed, but not obeyed; nay, obedience is counted as preciseness, and so reproached." He was deeply concerned, therefore, about awakening a sleepy generation of church-goers from their false sense of security. As a result, he labored to lead people into a well-grounded assurance of salvation.

To that end, Perkins produced several writings in which he explained how we are to search our consciences for the least evidence of salvation based on Christ's saving work. He viewed his efforts in this regard as part of a pastor's fundamental task in keeping "balance in the sanctuary" between divine sovereignty and human responsibility. Pastors had to demonstrate how God's immovable will moved man's will and how to look for evidence of inclusion in God's covenant. They also had to instruct their people as to how to make their election sure.

According to Perkins, one of the principal means by which God imparts assurance is the covenant of grace. The golden chain of salvation (predestination, calling, justification, sanctification, and glorification) is linked to us through the preaching God's gracious covenant. Perkins pointed to this covenant as a basis for assurance, maintaining that God becomes our God by means of the gracious covenant propounded in the gospel, promising pardon of sin in Christ.

As far as Perkins was concerned, we are active in terms of our covenant relation with God. Yet he acknowledged that we never glean assurance from a conditional covenant alone, for human conditionality can never answer all the questions conjoined with human depravity and divine sovereignty. For Perkins, the covenant also contains an absolute relationship. Assurance does not flow from the covenant's conditional nature, which is connected to our performance, but from the covenant's absolute nature, which is grounded in God's gracious being and promises. Perkins comments, "The promise is not made to the work, but to the worker, and to the worker, not for the merit of his work, but for the merit of Christ." Although Perkins encouraged people to strive after assurance, he ultimately pointed them to God's grace, declaring that the covenant itself is a divine gift rooted in Christ's merit. Assurance, in the final analysis, rests on God's faithfulness to His covenant promises, making even the fulfillment of the condition of faith on our part possible only by God's gracious gift.

Perkins understood that faith is a supernatural gift by which we take hold of Christ with all the promises of salvation. The object of faith is Christ alone. Faith first sees Christ as the sacrifice on the cross for the remission of sins, then learns to experience Him as the strength to battle temptation, the comfort to endure affliction, and ultimately as everything needed in this life and the life to come. In sum, faith shows itself when "every person particularly applies to himself Christ with His merits by an inward persuasion of the heart which comes no other way but by the effectual certificate of the Holy Spirit concerning the mercy of God in Christ Jesus."

Faith, therefore, has no meaning apart from Christ. "Faith is … a principal grace of God whereby man is engrafted into Christ and thereby becomes one with Christ and Christ one with him." Perkins's numerous references to faith as an "instrument" or "hand" must be understood in this context. Faith is a gift of God's sovereign pleasure that moves us to respond to Christ through the preaching of the Word. Perkins's use of the term "instrument" or "hand" conveys the simultaneously passive and active role of faith in this redemptive activity. Initially, faith is the passive "instrument" or "hand," granted by God to the sinner to receive Christ. Yet precisely at the moment when Christ is received, faith responds to the gift of grace. Thus, the response is most active when it has completely yielded to the person it has received. This concept of faith, within the context of covenant, is pivotal to Perkins's theology. His intense concern for the godly life arises alongside his equally intense concern to maintain the Reformation principle of salvation by grace alone, for we are never granted salvation on account of our faith but by means of faith.

Though the promises of God received by faith are the primary ground of assurance of faith, Perkins did not deny that a secondary ground of assurance, which flowed out of faith, involved the so-called practical syllogism. He wrote that assurance is "by little and little conceived in a form of reasoning or practical syllogism framed in the mind by the Holy Ghost." A believer can grow in assurance by reasoning this way: Only true believers hunger and thirst after Christ's righteousness. By the Spirit's grace, I cannot deny that I truly hunger and thirst after Christ's righteousness. Consequently, I may be assured that I am a child of God.

This kind of assurance, valid and helpful as it may be, is always dependent on the Spirit's illumination in the conscience to discern the work of God. Hence also this form of assurance accrues to a believer out of God's sovereign grace, and must always be grounded in Christ and His promises. Perkins wrote that this "assurance of conscience" may never be divorced from the work of the Spirit in prompting faith, for "the principal agent and beginner thereof, is the Holy Ghost, enlightening the mind and conscience with spiritual, divine light, and the instrument is the ministry of the gospel received by faith."

Perkins was committed to proclaiming this experience of God's sovereign grace from humiliation to assurance and seeing it cultivated in others. In his estimation, the Reformed theology of grace, the golden chain, was not a subject for mere academic debate and discussion, but was crucial to the development of true Christian piety. He was convinced that people must experience an affective appropriation of God's sovereign grace, moving beyond intellectual assent to heartfelt dedication to Christ.

This experimental piety earned Perkins the label *Puritan*. Strictly speaking, he was not a Puritan in terms of his ecclesiology, for he refused to align himself with the more militant figures of his era. Nor was he a Puritan in terms of his theology, for it is anachronistic to speak of Puritanism as a theological movement prior to the Arminian renewal in theology, which occurred within the Church of England during the reign of the Stuart kings. But Perkins was a Puritan in terms of his piety. "For the pure heart is so little regarded," says he, "that the seeking after it is turned to a by-word, and a matter of reproach. Who are so much branded with vile terms of *Puritans* and *Precisians* as those who most endeavor to get and keep the purity of heart in a good conscience?" Again, "The due obedience to the moral law is nick-named and termed preciseness, and the professors thereof called *Puritans* and *Precisians*, for this cause only, that they make conscience of walking in obedience to God's law."

Perkins would never have described himself as a Puritan, given its negative connotation, yet it is the very term that others used, favorably or not, to describe that experimental theology so prevalent in his life and ministry.

CONCLUSION

Few men have been as influential in their lifetime as William Perkins, and few men of such fame have been so widely forgotten with the passing of time as Perkins. While living, he published twenty-one books. After his death, these were frequently reprinted. Moreover, friends and students published twenty-seven new books in his name. These were edited from his many manuscripts. John Legate gathered Perkins's works into three volumes in 1608–9, and these were reprinted more than a dozen times. They were also translated into Latin and published as *Opera Theologica* eight times by 1668. At least fifty editions of Perkins's works were printed in Germany and Switzerland. There were 185 seventeenth-century printings of his individual or collected works in Dutch. Furthermore, his writings were translated into Spanish, Welsh, Irish, French, Italian, Hungarian, and Czech. The international popularity of Perkins's works led one biographer to declare that "his books spoke more tongues than the author ever knew."

In 1611, the East India Company issued a directive, according to which English agents working abroad were to receive copies of Richard Hakluyt's *Principal Navigations of the English Nation*, John Foxe's *Book of Martyrs*, and William Perkins's *Works*. The following annotation is included in the 1620 records of the Virginia Company of London:

> After the acts of the former court were read, a stranger stepped in presenting Sir Walter Raleigh's map, containing a description of Guiana, and great books, as a gift from someone who desired that his name should remain unknown. One of these books was St. Augustine's *The City of God*, while the other three volumes were the works of Mr. Perkins, newly corrected and amended. The donor desired that the books be sent to the college in Virginia, and remain there for the use of the collegiate.

In New England, close to one hundred Cambridge men, including William Brewster of Plymouth, Thomas Hooker of Connecticut, John Winthrop of Massachusetts Bay, and Roger Williams of Rhode Island, lived in Perkins's shadow. It has been said that "a typical Plymouth Colony library comprised a large and small Bible, Henry Ainsworth's translation of the Psalms, and the works of William Perkins, a favorite theologian." Richard Mather was converted while reading from Perkins, and—more than a century later—Jonathan Edwards was gleaning insights from Perkins's writings. One historian observes, "Anyone who reads the writings of early New England learns that Perkins was indeed a towering figure in their eyes."

In seeking to account for Perkins's popularity, one scholar identifies two unique features in his writings: first, "an ability to clarify and expound complex theological issues which aroused the respect of fellow scholars"; and, second, "a gift for relating seemingly abstruse theological teaching to the spiritual aspirations of ordinary Christians." To state it simply, Perkins was able to merge intricate theology with practical piety—a rare gift indeed. This made his writings very appealing to a large audience and, as a result, "no books were more often to be found upon the shelves of succeeding generations of preachers, and the name of no preacher recurs more often in later Puritan literature."

Perkins's legacy is multi-faceted. To begin with, he was instrumental in securing the Reformation in England. The English Reformation was a drawn out process, in which the country moved back and forth on multiple occasions between Roman Catholicism and Protestantism as monarchs came and went. In a span of twenty years, the religion of the land shifted four times. But the reign of Elizabeth brought stability, and provided the much-needed climate for English Reformers to solidify the church's position. Perkins played a pivotal role in this, and his works became the standard polemic against Roman Catholicism.

In addition to the English Reformation, Perkins made an incalculable contribution to the advancement of Reformed theology. Arminius's treatment of predestination was predicated on Perkins's writings. Samuel Ward and John Davenant, the English delegates at the Synod of Dort in 1618–19, championed Perkins's position. These factors ensured that the theological ideas at the heart of the debate belonged to Perkins. Unknown to him, he left a discernible imprint upon what are now called the five points of Calvinism

Thirdly, Perkins shaped the future of pastoral ministry on both sides of the Atlantic. His role as a physician of the soul became paradigmatic for succeeding generations of ministers. His emphasis on expounding the text, deriving doctrines from the text, and applying those doctrines through a multitude of uses, is clearly evident in the collected sermons of subsequent Puritan preachers. His method of preaching shaped the English pulpit well into the eighteenth century, and is still felt in some quarters of the church today

Fourthly, Perkins laid the foundation for the development of a distinct piety. Behind the industrious scholar, combative polemicist, exhaustive expositor, and prolific author stood a pastor deeply concerned about the spiritual condition of the individual in the pew. He was convinced that people must experience an affective appropriation of sovereign grace, moving beyond intellectual assent to heartfelt dedication to Christ. This experimental piety set the tone for the literature that would pour forth from the presses in the seventeenth century, thereby ensuring him a place in history as the father of Puritanism.

Finally, Perkins emphasized the centrality of Christ. In the words of one contemporary, "The scope of all Perkins's godly endeavors was to teach Christ Jesus and Him crucified, and to move all men to repentance." This is perhaps the most fitting legacy for a man whose greatest desire was to "preach one Christ by Christ to the praise of Christ."

BIBLIOGRAPHY

Peter Ackroyd, *Tudors: The History of England from Henry VIII to Elizabeth 1* (New York: Thomas Dunne Books, 2012).

Joel R. Beeke, *Assurance of Faith: Calvin, English Puritanism, and the Dutch Second Reformation* (New York: Peter Lang, 1991).

_____, "William Perkins on Predestination, Preaching, and Conversion," in *The Practical Calvinist: An Introduction to the Presbyterian and Reformed Heritage,* ed. Peter A. Lillback (Fearn, Ross-shire: Christian Focus, Mentor, 2002), 183–213.

Joel R. Beeke and J. Stephen Yuille, "Biographical Preface," in *The Works of William Perkins: Volume 1,* ed. J. Stephen Yuille (Grand Rapids: Reformation Heritage Books, 2014), ix–xxxii.

Joel R. Beeke and Mark Jones, *A Puritan Theology: Doctrine for Life* (Grand Rapids: Reformation Heritage Books, 2014).

Joel R. Beeke and Randall Pederson, *Meet the Puritans*

(Grand Rapids: Reformation Heritage Books, 2006), 469–480.

Ian Breward, "Introduction," *The Works of William Perkins*, ed. Ian Breward, The Courtenay Library of Reformation Classics (Appleford: Sutton Courtenay Press, 1970), 3.3–131.

_____, "The Life and Theology of William Perkins" (Ph.D., University of Manchester, 1963).

Benjamin Brook, *The Lives of the Puritans* (1813; repr., Morgan: Soli Deo Gloria, 1996), 2.129–136.

Samuel Clark, *The Marrow of Ecclesiastical History, Contained in the Lives of One Hundred Forty-Eight Fathers, Schoolmen, First Reformers, and Modern Divines* (London, 1654), 850–853.

Charles Cooper and Thompson Cooper, *Athenae Cantabrigiensis 1586–1609* (Cambridge: Deighton, Bell, and Co, 1861), 2.335–341.

Thomas Fuller, *Abel Redevivus: or, The Dead Yet Speaking. The Lives and Deaths of the Modern Divines* (London, 1651), 431–440.

_____, *The Holy State* (Cambridge, 1642), 88–93.

Lionel Greve, "Freedom and Discipline in the Theology of John Calvin, William Perkins, and John Wesley: An Examination of the Origin and Nature of Pietism" (Ph.D., Hartford Seminary Foundation, 1976).

Michael Jinkins, "William Perkins," *Oxford Dictionary of National Biography*, ed. H. C. G. Matthew and Brian

Harrison (Oxford: Oxford University Press, 2004), 43:781–784.

Sidney Lee (ed.), "William Perkins," *The Dictionary of National Biography* (London: Smith, Elder & Co., 1909), 15:892–895.

R. David Lightfoot, "William Perkins' View of Sanctification" (Th.M., Dallas Theological Seminary, 1984).

Coleman C. Markham, "William Perkins's Understanding of the Function of Conscience" (Ph.D., Vanderbilt University, 1967).

Donald K. McKim, *Ramism in William Perkins's Theology* (New York: Peter Lang, 1987).

Thomas F. Merrill (ed.), *William Perkins, 1558–1602, English Puritanist: His Pioneer Works on Casuistry: 'A Discourse of Conscience' and 'The Whole Treatise of Cases of Conscience* (Nieuwkoop: B. DeGraaf, 1966).

Charles R. Munson, "William Perkins: Theologian of Transition" (Ph.D., Case Western Reserve, 1971).

W. Brown Patterson, *William Perkins and the Making of a Protestant England* (Oxford: Oxford University Press, 2014).

William Perkins, *The Art of Prophesying,* ed. Sinclair Ferguson (Edinburgh: Banner of Truth Trust, 1996).

_____, *A Commentary on Galatians,* ed. Gerald T. Sheppard (New York: Pilgrim Press, 1989).

_____, *A Commentary on Hebrews 11,* ed. John H. Augustine (New York: Pilgrim Press, 1991).

_____, *The Works of William Perkins*, 3 vols. (London, 1631).

_____, *The Works of William Perkins,* gen. eds. Joel R. Beeke and Derek W. Thomas (Grand Rapids: Reformation Heritage Books, 2014ff.), volumes 1 and 2 of a projected 10-volume reprint.

Joseph A. Pipa, Jr., "William Perkins and the Development of Puritan Preaching" (Ph.D., Westminster Theological Seminary, 1985).

Victor L. Priebe, "The Covenant Theology of William Perkins" (Ph.D., Drew University, 1967).

Paul R. Schaefer, Jr., *The Spiritual Brotherhood: Cambridge Puritans and the Nature of Christian Piety* (Grand Rapids: Reformation Heritage Books, 2011).

Mark R. Shaw, "The Marrow of Practical Theology: A Study in the Theology of William Perkins" (Ph.D., Westminster Theological Seminary, 1981).

Rosemary Sisson, "William Perkins" (M.A., University of Cambridge, 1952).

Young Jae Timothy Song, *Theology and Piety in the Reformed Federal Thought of William Perkins and John Preston* (Lewiston, N.Y.: Edwin Mellen, 1998).

J. R. Tufft, "William Perkins, 1558–1602" (Ph.D., Edinburgh, 1952).

James Eugene Williams, Jr., "An Evaluation of William Perkins' Doctrine of Predestination in the Light of John Calvin's Writings" (Th.M., Dallas Theological Seminary, 1986).

J. Stephen Yuille, *Living Blessedly Forever: The Sermon on the Mount and the Puritan Piety of William Perkins* (Grand Rapids: Reformation Heritage Books, 2012).